MW01275730

promises

april's promises

Jerry Cordeiro

APRIL'S PROMISES

Published by Jerry Cordeiro, Edmonton, Canada

ISBN 0-978-1-77354-215-7

Publication assistance and digital printing in Canada by

PUBLISHING
PageMaster.ca

open me...
a book is the only thing that loves to get old
and in many years from now these pages that you revisit,
will have that one scent you once were in love with
old books
close me...

wind

i wanna be
the only one she loves...

~ap~

loving you was just an earlier heaven

~ap~

arrogance of love

love ain't for keeping...
so i know when to step away from storms
a seamstress who ties me along
patches me up but can rip my soul
she weaves patterns for a potential shield
wounded reds that scratches portray
you shall believe beyond this cloudy day
you sizzled me sooner than flames
so i smolder and wait
the sympathetic sway of the grass will drift on
stones at our feet will all be heart-shaped
but buried deep so your hands need to feel filth
i'm like an open book like the one i got you to read
i'm bound to fall through pages each chapter of us
the past is just a goodbye
the moment is always that hello
in tall grass or in the corner of a lonely cafe
my mind will follow
like a curious butterfly who appears to make it clear
we are only the ones who will lose
with the battle of fear
i'm singing wild
because the vanity of war
riddles my heart with every arrogance of love

~ap~

she walked away barefoot and eyes wet
saying to herself i dodged a bullet
i won't regret trampled daisies
sage and the smell of your neck
in gutters overseas, i was left shipwrecked
how come a spider never gets caught on her own trap
cause the fellow fly is craving the weakness of the sap
i wonder how much you would desire me
if you loved as though you were never hurt
by loves consequences my fallen petal i gave
are embedded in our dirt...

~ap~

i would have loved you until death
but you killed my heart to save yours
from the fucking nightmare of losing me

~*ap*~

but i'm a wild crazy girl
and i'm led by wind, struggle and pain
the only thing that is certain
is that i'll crave the death of your memory
and the birth of tired eyes
the way i exhaust all possibilities
and squish the relentless attempts
to love this wild tangled man
i'm held together by one string only
tug, yank and pull
that's how i know my heart is pushing back
please don't wait too long
cause you will lose nothing less than everything...

~ap~

angel despite

i thought you were different from all those other eyes
i never let you completely in
because i had a feeling it was a disguise
as you stepped over diamonds
avoiding the evade of your sight
the devil on your shoulder befriends the angel despite
i wondered why he didn't love me
was it the words i could not release
was it that i didn't let him in
to take the only broken piece
i think now i figured it out
why it wasn't him
he just couldn't give it all to someone
what he didn't have within...

~ap~

at night when your thoughts are your own
i'll be under the same emptiness of this sky
i burrow up with my own arms squirming
in only short memories that get eaten up
by your vicious appetite to shatter me
each piece of the mirror ricochets
the desire to be a good lover
but i can't help but squeeze the shards
to feel the assurance of wounded eyes
could it ever be as good again
like the first time my wet mouth landed on your upper lip
like a daddy long leg spider tiptoeing on my window's pane
do you ever care to look inside
the only one i was most comfortable with
saw the darkest side of me

i realize i couldn't ever keep you cause you weren't mine
so i let go for as long as it takes to fly around
searching for you again in someone else's skin
i don't want to know the reasons why we didn't try
i don't want to know what i said
to make you let go and not look back
i know now how death tastes like
it's cold, bitter and hard to swallow
so i stopped breathing, just to hear if you're in that whisper
i guess i love you cause i need to
please take this charm of mine i pour into words
fidget with it so you know you are sure
i'll be a wishing star in the same sky we both belong to
sitting quietly alone in a rocking chair
lost in our own space
inside midnight and underneath the blackness
of my heart

~ap~

angel tears in my jar help me live
it bandages my heart with each song
when all dull clouds imitate my imitation of laughter
i stop the beating and seal it airtight
i was disguising when you found me
and my doors were fastened shut
i let no one in, i keep all curtains closed
with a tiny space to peak
no tomorrows just yesterday's glint
will be my companion until her, until you
i will answer my own questions
and ask what i already know
i will be kind, thoughtful
and i'll share my air until i noticed
the inhalation of a selfish pulse
at night it will be hard
the anguish of our beat
every single pound will be heard
until my chest is concave and dark
there will still be life
between a minuscule of relief and regret
i disguise again what my heart relied on
so i glance occasionally to the window
where i see all your secrets in the stars and the lies in the sky
so i will remain here, put away and kept safe
waiting for heaven to make my angel weep

~ap~

ruin me only from inside
my character
a frantic gull ripping breath
in each stroke of her butterfly wings
i clench and press down her mouth
with pressure of my hand
just letting enough air to be sucked
i pulled it out already with the hand she couldn't hold
we flail into a slither and in between pain
until i agonize her anatomy again and again
her greeting is wet floors
wet walls and dry thoughts
like a desert abandoned
where vultures pretend to weep for the moisture of a cry
ravening for the last two pieces of flesh
i eat until i finish
leaving bones and stones unturned...

~*ap*~

i held on this last tear that you forced out of my eye
i hold it up high and let it fall gently
like a warm blanket forgotten in the sun
i know now why the caged birds weep
those wings bond tight, confined to fallacy and strain
agony settles in like a grip from an eagle
the affliction of injury is altered
from the beauty of being dragged through clouds
you clipped too short
and i forgot i once was in love with soaring
i started to wilt away to sleep
another hundred more dawns
without the feeling of morning
and springs render
you often leave the cage ajar
in hoping that my curiosity doesn't venture too far

april's promises

i didn't want to go but my dreams collapsed
in the heavy rain, you disguised as tears
while i listen to the ocean crashing through
all my innocence are folded in few
you again left the door unburdened and i took the chance
my wail was fierce and frantic
i knew then it was for good
but remember you lion tamer
i was not meant to be caged
i was not meant to be cultivated into shape
don't lock up something that you wanted inside your hands
these hands now wave goodbye...

~ap~

jerry cordeiro

little boy, why do you push
i was told my heart was broken into two
one side is as black as a starless sky
blacker than a pirate's patch
angered from the spear in his eye
the other side the most beautiful red
a deep passionate shade
that demands attention from wounds
from a thorn on a rose to blossom again
i throb with pain of missing you
i haven't washed you off my skin yet
for the worry of not getting another chance
to quench my thirsty mind
i cannot count how many times i've tossed you from my raft
to protect my heart from drowning
there are a billion smiles in this world
but yours kills them all
like shots fired they enter me like healing arrows
and the bullets fall to my knees like tears
we end up searching our whole lives for souls like ours
but my garbage pollutes our ground we tiptoe on
what happened to the little boy whose smile
was genuine and his circumstances were out of his control
he didn't get taught to smile alone but to trip and roll
so mother if you're listening remind me of him
so father if you're listening fuck you, from him

~ap~

16

i forgot how cruel the world was when you passed my glance
i envy the mirror for the privilege it has to see you
i'm a fool for love when you danced in my eyes
you are my words i cannot write
if my wings should fail me
send me walking towards your steps
for one brief spell, i'd cast one hundred regrets
to see you one last time in the minutes before i left
i must taste the bitterness to get to the sweeter parts
where i'll continue to dream of fucking you

~ap~

pluck...

how subtle did my memory erase
my aching touch longed to trace
the folding sky influenced my ways
that one beautiful daisy with one petal left remained
come home to my arms stretched and firm
my hurried love is impatient to fill
to breathe some softened strain
i may not have been all i've shown
my heart was full of emptiness
that one more tear would overfill it
to sympathy with hope of all my forgotten dents
i once again scattered flowers
and properly traced my yearning
i held tight and i strangled all chances of release
my love was hidden in dust
all thoughts and strangulating knots

all those letters that never did reach you
i foreplay with ink and i fuck my words
on paper like white linen sheets
feathers and a velvet tongue
i caught all smiles and stole your laughter
the guilty robber pours forth in gushes
i listened underneath the songs that flood my limits
and everything billows and falls in grieving sleeps
you disappear slowly
and the fades that last long enough to smear
keep secrets smouldering and near
your footsteps find echoes of my directions that remain
and today, yesterday and tomorrow i throw away hours
and days multiplied with unanswered wounds
my tangled brain is stuck among pages of silent beats
today i pluck that last petal...

~ap~

i am him
i am her
i am cohen
i am no cure
i am atticus
i am frost
i am polo
i'm not lost
i am atticus
he is me
cohen does the singing
hoar frost solicits the tree...

~ap~

i am jealous the wind
gets to push through your hair
and the trees are left
with the smell of your subtle sway
i fell for you the same way you fall asleep
restless, careful, slowly, then all at once...

~*ap*~

the broken glass that cut your hand
was a reminder that we bleed
the blood that surfaced out of your wound
was a reminder that we need
the broken girl that hides inside is terrified of this boy
the reflection of the women now believes
that love is just a toy
the broken pieces that we tried to puzzle back
are scattered from being tossed
the chances of finding someone so close
will never ever be crossed

~ap~

free to be me

i'll gallop as long as it takes
a chance is all i run towards
she doesn't know how much i loved her
how everything i ever wanted was that
it is subtle how misery loves company
and even with a full choir, i forget the chorus
i loved the way i felt when i was near her
when i loved her, i needed her
i sure know what sadness looks like
how it steals the breath like a forest fire
where trees scream to be left to dance
i came along not by accident
i was led by angels that knew i needed those wings
mine broke off and fell while i soared
in the eye of sins and storms
all those birds that fly above me chirp and sing
they all know what makes me hum
but they are not you
if you came to fix me, you'd leave by the morning anyway
is it worth these bullet holes
is it worth two lost souls
is it worth the freedom...

~ap~

you left before i had a chance to play my entire song...

~*ap*~

between me it should be you, and in you, i could only be...

~ap~

inside my broken window

i need sun
i don't do well in the dark
you with eyes like soft clouds
i tend to stare for hours
and picture you left on an island
i cannot leave you
i must drift on sticks and stones
but words are what hurt me
my dreams are what keeps me swimming
lonely gaze along with breath on my shoulders
makes me feel you without the arrogance of touch
i stop all other noises and let the world wonder why
the signs are clear
they are not bright letters but feather thin

while the chances make our two hearts taper into one
do we need something beautiful to die
so our faith remains broken
when my eyes close to finish the day's glare, you is what i find
your blue windows i see the true colour
hidden from the outside
i see all the way through like no other
inside genie bottles, wishing wells and falling stars
i wished for you and i will continue to skip stones
a broken window i prefer to look in
so the shards find their way deeper...

~*ap*~

jerry cordeiro

i once lived in him quietly
to the eyes of others
and deafening amidst his skin
burn until you wince
unearth my winds
for that is the only cure to ease
i must teach my feet to fly
i've walked through thousands of clouds pushing them aside
like mouthfuls of kisses, inside cotton candy
i searched, it seems like forever
i got so close to his breath, but whispers guided me lost
he let go, like a pebble of pollen chipped off a drunken bee
his honey i collected, feeds all my gust
and i feel seized by the web and gripped by fangs
now the hunger of thirst and its douse of poison
leaves me deserted
in the despair of destiny's demise...

~ap~

when i hold you again
i'm not letting you slip through my hands
i will make sure i show you
how desperate my empty palms
need that skin under my nails
like sand and all those million pieces
i'll touch every single one intentionally
leaving parts of me scattered
those stones skip through puddles tears deep
i'll try catching the wind
but those gifts shouldn't be held
just felt
every stitch threaded between my seams
your presence blankets my rest
i'll wait for you
and that's when i will finally sleep
under dreams and through clouds
all those whispers, my ears will finally know
you are all my body needs
and now
i realize the meaning of thirst...

~ap~

it is like you set me on fire...
all those old branches have scorched to only dust
where i can see myself run free
like a blade of grass, i yawn with my eyes shut tight
and eager to see you in an instant
you lift me up before i wilted away
to sleep another hundred dawns
without the feeling of spring
i feel like a fire lily
i stand up firm and i stretch my petals wide
i wait for your drops to flow over my ridge
and into my stream, we will soak
i need that fresh air to awake my stillness
i know that it is no way for a heart to beat
but without us it's like being alone deep inside a song

where the birds never rest
is where wishes care to hum you safe
with the breeze, all my innocence are folding few
because i daydream of all the secrets
and things i assume you would do to me
i ricochet you in my mind
and i lay that kiss you left me
gently on the ground where i rest
how awful of me to create any other feeling
but only to crave your warmth
i am only comfortably drowning without us
and only you can save me
when you cry, i believe
when you dream, i will learn how
so set me on fire cause i will burn those layers
until i find that touch
and then i will begin to grow...

~*ap*~

wrong oceans

we are adrift anchored in wrong oceans
but the waves still crash and corrode
nobody can take the pain away from me cause it is mine
your karma is shaped into sharp stones
and the diamonds you once wore
bludgeoned my vision of you
all layers of tears you spun weaves through lashes
your eyes strike as deep as you can
when you come undone who can repair
but a carpenter's daughter with no love she is willing to spare
now i'm defending myself with cages
gathering wings for pillows so my dreams can learn to fly
with the desire so blind
i would have been everything you wanted to see
revenge renders you the ability to be real
and necessity to be me
as all my words fall into place
and slowly fuck into a relation of gravity
and an alliance to god
i've waited by the ocean window
hoping you would be on the edge of my pain

telling me all the reasons
why you should of never let me leave your arms again
together we were everything that love should die for
but apart we killed wishes that the creator put in place
stars were aligned to show us our way
two lonely boats lost at sea
and it was us that were placed, aloft in hurt
so now through the night's darkness
my heart still calls to her
i wonder if she will ever answer my cry
or will she drown all the reasons
and settle for the island of why
she came in the shape of magic
and the smoke and mirrors gave it away
she looked exactly like art
and reminded me how butterflies are painted
and now i stare at an empty canvas
with less words drowning me like deep water...

~ap~

past my control

spoiling the colours as yellow eats into the leaves
each petal ends in an edge of beauty
and i lie here thinking that something will be found
as our hearts rose through
my eyes recoiled with broken despair
my stretched arms with hands seeking
i dug deep and found
i now grown beneath the bridges i have torn
my sore feet throughout blistering years
and by day a cloud would do
shadowing my faraway glimpse of breath astray
when on my trail i have forgotten how to cry
reliving the emotions once known
a hundred dawns i have wasted
for all the beauty that night takes away
for every hour of shine there follows one more of tears

my paces strutted back with fading stars
and a choking flame mutters chance
shadows float before my eyes responded wet
overgrown inside a hundred mazes
each step distressed patterns and abstract my notion
i love the very clear truth
if only your devoted eyes would offer a drop
the days now of past are fled
and a bare stage where the curtain calls my shades in place
i battle to find the truth, in lying colours painted blue
the frozen feathers chip slowly
and silt remains unknown
as my dreams resume lower than my child's glint
my bad dreams will be written far past my control

~ap~

her dance i hum
inside a careless
kitchen waltz
with fretless jazz
she sang me into the blues
tied in her
lonesome chords
i witnessed her
secret notes
written in
harmony to kill
the poets' strum

~ap~

it was in that moment
how i just knew
my life would never be
the same
between a latte and a tea
we were forever meant to be...

~*ap*~

jerry cordeiro

my heart recognized you
quicker than my eyes could focus
upon opening them i knew
my idea of what love is was forever fucked...

~ap~

i'll never love you more than tomorrow

~ap~

apple tree

i was burned into Halloween orange
with cherry lip gloss and strawberry lips
her tangerine juices waterboarded me into confessions
her chipped halo bound with thorns
cultivated an appetite in which she knew me so well
you've been reading my mail from raccoon scratches
that left my plastic regrets unable to recycle
the cycle of my pain
she planted seeds where the roots gather to chat
a coffee shop and under skies is where we started that
for now, this rain collected elsewhere
i drought in floods of desires
i try to convince myself of love
i'll settle for a lonely poet's paradise
in shade under the poetry of my apple tree

~ap~

crying is the end of all feelings
and tears are only left
so you can learn
from the slippery floors

~ap~

dead flowers...

i was lost to the sensitivities of love
and now i spend all hours confused with why
you can tell if he loves you by the way he kissed
at times it would imitate
like fingerprints pressed so deliberate
in which no other could replace
when i felt him my identity was languages
melted into desire's ribcage
it was easier to kill it with hate
and in a crowd is where i'd blush
everyone who sees my telling eyes would know
they must be lovers of abandonment
and somehow they aren't letting it form they would say
the creator grins her teeth
and when god was giving away trueness to a lonely pillow
it was them that defined it and finally fell asleep
waking up and reaching over
on my side of warmth

lying to the heart in between the night's darkness
is where our tears will call back to him
i'll hope he answers my cry
and if i ever figure out how to just keep him tangled in two
i will gather all vines and roots
so we could have a garden to feed our souls
on the heals of wounds we would live forever
in my tiny home
where the birds have a plethora of voice
to sing me in and out of love
for myself to find my own wild horse
to tame him into confession
so i will learn how to be free
to be me...

~*ap*~

needless compromise

he promised the world
then i lived for him
a lifetime pledge
etched in every contour
of every letter that words battled
in a carnage of vows
the brokenness of his spine
wove exactly like her path of dalliance
the softness of her sashay
seems to sail in a solitude of soothe
there is nothing like it in days
yesterdays try to impress
she promised him death
then he rose from thorns
each time she left him grounded
a lifetime plight scratched
in every corner of his journey of kiss

~*ap*~

bridge

i'll be forever not far away
just under your pillow for you to taste me today
at least i was the one that hurt you the most
that felt you up the most
that kissed you in every hole
every room, under your skin
beneath white sheets stained by the moon
there were the eyes that fell away
from your once entrenched heart
by giving me your broken puzzle
and by you not giving me the last part
when you dream there are no lies
like a widow in the dark you must ease into fear
anxious and all its subtleties
each goosebump knows my name and smell
no way to ever disappear
with carpenter hands he carved my eyes
so trust would build walls
instead of the bridges of madness carnality

~ap~

i stretched for you

and the elastics around my heart frayed into a soft fade

i'm now restless in a pursue of my blue veins

that finally touches true air and spills into red

love was the easy part of you

but all comforts we enjoyed

was like an anchor at the bottom of the sea

holding us from storms above

instead of letting us be wild and free

we should have been like a terrified leaf

afraid from the fall

and all seasons without us...

~ap~

what if a poet has written exactly
what i needed to say?
how dare they get away
with the plagiarism of my pain...

~*ap*~

adrift

temporarily lost at sea
how can i find what i already had
that was everything i ever needed
to find wind that could love me all up
when my breeze feels down
i must learn to rest
for the rest of my horizon
so i lay my head and i begin
somehow, i can still smell you
my pillowcase remembers making it rain
but it's the tears that have stayed and remained
my fingers like tree branches
pressed against my own throat and neck
for this desire you leaving me adrift won't ever wreck
your inner thighs are like sandcastles
slowly losing their form
one tiny stone, one subtle groan
clay in my hands i mold my sway
to fit perfectly inside the tide
changing every shoreline
each wave brings sins to your sail
and i anchor deep

my island is here with you
and i deserted from wanting any other shooting star
because you have been my wish
a million kisses that seep
like the blush of a young bride you leave me
like they all left me
my only defence is colour
my wings clipped, eyes fastened tightly in a soft gentle fall
my hands are carved from a father's calloused comfort
a carpenter with rusted nails
digging in the panes of all windows
his shattered pieces are used to rip me
i'll try to do different mistakes
with a broken heart that can still love
until then come haunt me and i'll love you wild
and i'll pray for your tame embrace
all i have left are my black eyes, sad eyes, cold eyes,
hungry eyes, lying eyes, bedroom eyes,
faraway eyes, hollow eyes, shallow eyes
and your eyes will always
remain adrift

~ap~

jerry cordeiro

what if we forget?
will we ever learn
how it felt?

~ap~

i caged him because i was afraid
of how high we could have flown
he once gave me my wings
but my fear left him behind bars
unwilling to climb...

~ap~

could i ever forgive myself
for that one split moment
i knew i was forever needing you?

~ap~

if u lose me
just know i will make love to u still
with ink
ache
and all the fucken letters
of every language
our tongues forgot to remind us

~ap~

you are chipped and torn
just like me
and just like me
i won't stop trying to fly wild
dreaming far
and sipping on your wine-stained lips
because i'm intoxicated
with your rainbow on my rainy daze...

~ap~

new years

take my lips...
i'll never use them again
take my eyes...
they are dried like a desert of a deserted destination
but i'm taking my black heart
feeding it now
polishing it to its finest shade
because black makes love to midnight
and at midnight the new year kisses me
with a whisper you couldn't take

~ap~

she hesitated
and i knew the answers where wishes changed
i counted a hundred times each word she threw
dropped to the bottom, deeper than oceans
farther then wounds could ever heal
she didn't know that under that murky water
lay treasures of a man that dares to love
like a pirate ready to see with both eyes

~*ap*~

if you had one more tear left inside of you...
would you bring me back to life?
this dried flower can't grow
without your weeps tangled in my roots...

~*ap*~

loving you was the easiest thing i've ever done...
but fuck, i never do take the easy way...

~ap~

love and lines

i disappeared inside you
but you struggled to see
that time was the only thing wasted
ricocheting love inside of me
being alive means
you are not afraid to love something
where silence isn't lonely anymore
cause you know the sound of his breath
she is and he will always be just a simple wish away...

~ap~

if only i could have shown
how strong my love was for her
a broken soldier
with bullets instead of kisses
i shot her down while she flew
her wings worn like skin
while her attempt to love me
scratched only the surface
she was my angel
i was her belief...

~ap~

fear holds the last two hearts captive
his and hers
she will eventually find
and his dark eyes will too
but she will never know the meaning
of that encounter of magic
because just a block away
wrote her entire new life...

~*ap*~

what is your paradise?
is it flying on a steel horse
or laying in the tall grass
under the same sky as me?

~ap~

i wonder what you look at
when you stare out the window
it is a sin for beauty to sleep alone
because dark hides what other hearts need to see...

~ap~

i can't seem to wash you off my skin as hard as i try
i rehearse what i would do to your body
in all my thoughts ahead
i send you my words from the corners of my lips
and then through windows i release them
i let go all those chances i need again to breathe you
i sit here watching the world turn
while you make mine stop still
we are staring at the same sky
and i send you a wink from a star
and in return i ask you to lay your imagination
between the softest of clouds
and inside the purest form of love
stop searching
it's me you've been looking for...

~ap~

what would i do without
as the dawn charges straight for today
i'll streamline to your wishes
so the chances you'll fly away would be plucked
you are something familiar that i haven't seen for a while
the smell on my fingers linger when i press them to my face
for the perfume is making my head assume
let it be mine
of all the things that songs are formed from
a sitting sparrow whistles
someday
someday
when my walk nears you
it's like freshness of newly turned earth
or rain when it washes restless leaves
we would make them dance
like old roses that have a new home
from tired love
to awaking lust
when the last few brittle attempts hold so tight
for the possibilities of falling into the right hands
it was meant for reasons love could only explain
between me
it should be you
and in you
i could only be

~ap~

follow me to all my words
i will continue to romanticize my attempts
and picture how easy it would be
in a quaint hold which your arms are pressured to release
i barely caught a glimpse of what could be tasted
you keep me wanting and i can't forget now
i'm letting my brain slip in places i thirst for
i often look at your hands
and know where they've been on my body
like roots digging in soil trying to get dirtier and deeper

~ap~

if my lips can't speak
if my eyes can't water
if my feet can't prove
what my heart can't alter
if my intentions are true
but my ways are shards of glass
and learning to be a good man
when bad was always the past
will dreams come true
in my own bubble view
if only you were placed in a broken down sailboat
on the side of no stream
to adventures no one would understand
the shine of our gleam

~ap~

puff

i held you so hard
and i treated you the same way
because just like a broken leaf
i've learnt to flutter
i've learnt how to catch ahold
of wind and replant
i will crumble
but i will grow
so be careful what you wish for
the lords of love are impatient
i'm left now certain
that i will gaze at the sky
why we didn't make the effort
now the wind will tell me
all the places you pass

i will be minding my own business
and suddenly your perfume
will interrupt my growth
you left so many secrets
deep to protect you inside
and i left all mine
in possibilities of true romance
true souls and the answers
that love demands
so let it sink in
don't huff and puff
and blow our love down...

~*ap*~

the smell of your neck
admiring can hurt in a brand-new breath
where kisses from your mouth
make broken look beautiful...

~ap~

once again

i realize no one will ever replace
and in return i can't shut the night off
your breath is intermingled with wind
and it insists on messaging my dreams
i am struggling against uncertain binds
opening like a book i find no release to fix my secret
i will eventually forget
and the gash across my heart
will hear my dreams eating the night
above avenues dust accepts the dryness of ground
the beauty mourns of narrow rumors beyond tomorrow
my lone heart that feeds off you
permanently reveals itself underneath ashes
as you go so i must
my life needs your smile
it breathes the air that leaves breath stirring in its blossom
it shatters wings that try to fly farther than we could soar
i will picture us finding each other where oceans kiss skies
i will look at you and then you will know
we are free
once again

~ap~

jerry cordeiro

i can feel you without touching you
i can taste honey without getting stung
i can slip into love without tears at my feet
i must get used to this rain
because it washes your scent
while concealing my truth...

~*ap*~

i love your secret and what i assume you're actually craving

~ap~

could your mouth ever forgive you
if you decide to actually stay gone
from the press of my lips?

~ap~

your drop

believe me when i say
to all reasons i cannot undo them
i have fear for saving the heart
cause all i have ever had was what i already knew
no cries no more can soak
the spills of painful attempts to love you properly
things i would share with you
no one could ever spare
like souls and dreams that collide
knowing within myself the pieces
i would give for you to use
to build whatever and whoever broke you before me
into my being i would lick your salt that each tear left
and replace those drops with my water
we would sail away forever and now
what promises that you guard can you release to me
so i can reassemble my tongue in languages
i've already spoke of
just know what flowers need
and just understand what i also need

~ap~

like a child's imagination
i pretend that it was meant for reasons
that love could only explain
it was us
under the oak tree
planning our adventure
of dancing in rainstorms
warm blankets under stars
and now as an old man or woman
imagination is my only reason

~*ap*~

i once lived in her heart
a red door and the greenest yard to lay on
each shadow from the tiny blades of grass
were so eager for us to walk barefoot on
they all knew we were nature
they understood that we were just like them
living life in a field of millions
each one so different
and each sway of the hearts beat
as certain as we would always be
free to be me

~ap~

lashes reopen in the middle of flight
to flee would only explain
look me diagonal and straighten my staggered shoes
my crazy love tightened like a straitjacket
cold and sleeveless tricks
the winds demand the truth of my skeptical life
on the shoulder of breath
i left from the window that birds rehearsed
would you still try to find me
and kiss my eyes for lost dreams are at stake
i hesitate to exist on different shades of black

~*ap*~

be afraid and do it anyways...
this elder once said to me
i repeated it
at every moment
i was just about to jump
into an adventure

~ap~

jerry cordeiro

you again...

i've seen you change into a butterfly
with white feathers being dropped at my feet
i've seen myself contort into an animal not seen in books
i felt the life and the true inhale when you passed me by
while the smell of your hair made my eyes shut softly
you forget in only days that i was the one wiping those eyes
reminding magic of its belief
your sorry eyes cried in pale blue
as mine, dark, endless and full of things you only knew
we end up making it alive from the war against our love
we fought for all the sins to understand
we survived because love was all we had and all we let go
in a constant attempt your words like bullets
failed to understand the direction of a butterfly...

~ap~

let your loss be your lesson
as i visit you at night
inside your dreams
i will teach you about truth
because true love
is always searching as well
wishing among all your tossing
of stones shaped in letters
now left behind is a bird without song
trying to remember
but neither of us was wrong
but we all know you can't change time
by holding all those seconds
minutes, hours and days
they all surface when dawn
taunts the arrival of an agonizing crave
i love you but you haven't been taught
to breathe forever

~ap~

if you deny true love
the hurt is yet to arrive
you spend days missing
and learning the definition of deprive...

~*ap*~

where do u go when u fall asleep?
i myself seem to go
wherever u last left me...

~ap~

i miss you
every inhaled moment your breath isn't in my space...

~ap~

when i kissed her
she put her hand on my chest
she knew i was him
she knew that years ahead
would be nothing less than a war zone
and only a paradise
if she dodged
the casualties of others' bullets

~ap~

jerry cordeiro

rain washes the restless leaves
and they dance like old roses
that have a new home...

~ap~

on my knees
her lips tasted like tangerines
and her mouth like hunger...

~ap~

i took a course called love
i aced with flying colours
my loves ended up being my lessons
i majored in the science of fear
i wasn't scared to fail
i ended up repeating all grades
and received my doctorate in the loneliness of love

~*ap*~

sometimes you get lucky in life
and end up finding a soul
that runs in fields like wild horses
we would be old souls with young eyes
feeling every whisper that our dreams scream out
we fight like eagle claws
ripping flesh in fear of getting lost alone...

~ap~

jerry cordeiro

you stole my love
like a thief attempts
to say sorry

~ap~

april's promises

storms

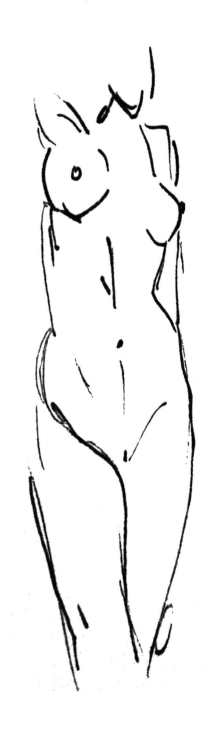

he walks away into the wind
and takes everything but my loneliness
so now i know he was not true
by the way you wouldn't drive in storms
no more will to hold until forever
those eyes are deeply dried
from attempts to tempt
from lies to love's disguise
there was nothing left to lose when you were mine
i felt at times i was close
to having my everything at every time
you always were flying in all directions but me
perhaps it was the times you had it all taken away
or all the promises they didn't keep for only you
you lost him you fool
he is gone now
like death's exhale
some ocean, partly sky, all heart
he is gone
you always knew he wouldn't do
that's why he felt it
like waves never the same
crashing against time

~*ap*~

timeless pearl...

i know our stars will meet above
our wings are different
but we fly to find love
i allowed my kiss
to fall between the strain of losing you
and while my tears drench
that is exactly what i've done so true
when my chances were mine, i fucked them deep
i didn't prove how soul mates are special and unique
my heart wasn't fixed
but you gave up not seeing my prime
again and again, i still fall in love every single time
with the thought of you just being my girl
because together we are the rarest diamond
and the purest timeless pearl...

~ap~

the calluses on my heart
are like the hands of a carpenter
scorched with the pain of words
embedded deep from years of pounding
i fly envious of time
but weary of the heights you constantly drop me from
your awfully clever attempts to break me
sliver in pieces i leave inside
for the reminder of sorrow
and the clarity of ache
you build my house of cards
placing them softly in order of my fates demise
lord... my world must come down so i can crawl
and learn the struggle of walking
on broken shells tossed at sea
on this empty island, i drift, i will learn to prey
i will instinctively learn to rip and tear that fake love
on paper, i send messages in bottles or screens
over your shoulder, the smell of me will appear
you will swallow and in each gulp you will be reminded
that callused broken heart could have been moistened
it could have been understood
it could have been forever
so now, fucken weep and pretend it doesn't hurt
because i am a carpenter's son
and i learnt how to pull nails out of my own flesh...

~*ap*~

jerry cordeiro

i must let you go if you're always trying to break me
hope died like crumbling wildflowers
you once gathered from my trail
the purity of pain
of each piece dusted into memories of cries
i clench my eyes to refrain from the anguish
the thistles caught beneath my skin
dirty time left slowly in seconds of filth
as you singed each minute
to eliminate my hand's ability to touch your face
you won't ever forget me
i will stretch and bind where agony is unkind
and the older you'll get the farther i'll fall behind
she had her own reasons why she wouldn't love me
now, as hard as i try, i could never make her cry
i held you for a little while
until your breath replied come back
after all, your words were like holding flames
and sharp knives in my back
to all those times my fingers left puddles under our feet
to all those times my tongue danced to the songs of moans
my familiar beat
i'll keep the truth alive in lonely hours
against ignorance and hate
with sorrow for a dream that's done
it is farewell to the journey
and saying fuck you to fate

~ap~

my oh my

my kindness ended up being your weakness
my weakness ended up being your cruelness
my wishes ended up being my heart's stitches
my wounds you ignored, left me in ditches
my screams for you to come back
my eyes saw true colours of the love you lack
my hands forgot what you feel
my plans and dreams a mirage that isn't real
my pain, your gain
my strain, your vain
my desire now soars higher
my broken wings
my queen with a dead king
my soul mate is gone
my fault, your fault, everyones wrong
my lies
my tries
my oh my

~ap~

you, like a tattoo...
if fate kissed lips, dreams end up finding themselves
i've been loving you too long to stop
i've stopped to love, far too long to have been nothing
how deep can this cut invade for my anguish
my hidden cries and lonely heart to cascade
your tears never got a chance to drown
i caught them all before they hit
i cry out to the night with you to blame
only the dancing shadows
of the leaves between the sun are my friends
just like a drug, i crave you
just like a drug, i need you
i can't stop forgetting that urge
when you fill my veins full of lies
that i was all you needed
all you dreamed of
all you wished for
how can i even believe a beautiful song again

when the melody melts into malice
and i begin to withdrawal
why aren't you coming for me
i hate you, but i love you even more
the ache is better than the coming
how it remains to hurt with time as it's fucking slowly
last night feels like a lifetime ago
when i decided to stop you from being able to hurt me again
you consumed me like fire
like the sound leaves make in wind storms
like the last breath of life you so effortlessly absorb
life now isn't what it seems
i'm a new creature
i will persevere, i will keep changing, i will be me
just know, i love you every single time i don't hate you
and forever i will have you in my imagination
and my skin like a tattoo...

~*ap*~

my lips

my need for licking between your hips

my wonder, what is she thinking

my mind, my worst enemy, stop drinking

my road now must fork

my blood, your wine must cork

my sorries

my glories

my web

my nest

my new her

my forever regret

~*ap*~

out of the cage i flew straight in the eye of storms
now is the most time i'll ever get back
so the chance will be taken
and on clouds, journeys will be formed
i'm like a widow
alive only in shell
buried deep
on shores with one set of footprints
they eventually wash clear of traces of you
carve glass that used to cut wounded hands
i was not a bird
but you fooled me in using your wings
to fly in directions of smoke without flames
on either side of these walls
i would never overlook those kind hands
because you helped find me, find myself...

~ap~

i must leap from nails pressed in my ribs
by lies you used to build our home
i thought you were him...
and only you were the one that could unbreak my heart
did you really love me
i whisper that to my own ears in silence i wait...
a thousand dreams i crushed by my own hands
and i held you so gentle at times
when love was a luring bird
and all songs seem to manifest our desires to be us
i slightly close my blind eyes shut in preparation
i still feel weak at the wings
on knees tired and bruised i beg
like hungry men i photograph
in hopes you'd find a shelter my transient heart could rest
but now you weakened me still
it was your smile that devoured my impression of bravery

i melt like puddles and drip like ice from your cold
those drops from the sides of your legs
i salivate from the image stuck in my iris
the taste becomes a need
as sun breaks in when things are right
i let the breeze determine my soul's direction
with windows left open
for trust must make its way out
i would have loved you till the ends of beginnings
from lust to rust
drowning only to save you from old waters
anchored at bottoms of your repair
only now dust will settle
as your fingers smear
you will remember that i existed...

~*ap*~

jerry cordeiro

sorry eyes
cried i
pouring to complete
i try
i go where broken is beautiful
her soft smile looking coy
i suffocate at the heart's pit
with lullabies
and all the pretty words i can imagine
i grow pale at the waves of lost love
gentle as a rose
as dead as dust
i'll wait as long as forever

~ap~

i'm inclined to tears
descending to alleviate how your words convey
for my moments to unfold i close my blinds
and my empty chairs articulate my patterns
all my restless sleeps
and heart stained worries are drenched when you go
i carried malice
and threw away letters to batter
a painter's mistake, an artist's agony will keep me sculpting
i will mold my dreams still
i will write all those words your body has ached for
so let your skin burn, let those spots i've tasted throb
it's quiet where my journeys end
rested upon hairs on the back of your neck
i keep searching for lower ground
to a mirage of damp arousal
i'll slither my hands overtop the grass with eyes closed
i'll rise to flames and shear all flowers to seeds
to once again use in my garden of plenty...

~ap~

i swallowed
unrecognized
for the amount of love
i had for her
she won't
recognize me now
because true love
can't be
discovered
where it didn't exist
inside her
worth of me
if you're out
there my gypsy
dance in the
rainstorms
so we can
disguise those tears
they made
us choke on...

~*ap*~

poetry of pain

analytical to my uniqueness
critical to my weakness
cynical to my brokenness
political to my petition
hypocritical to my intuition
sodomitical to my restriction
radical to your senses
sociable to my expenses
identical to my offences
impractical to my consequences
historical to our chain
egotistical to your gain
logical to my brain
lyrical to the poetry of pain...

~*ap*~

production of love...

like a marionette with jointed limbs
i've been manipulated into submission
for the purpose of loves debt with karma
my open arms subdued and chastened by strings
threaded by years of yearn
i've seemed to be waiting a lifetime
to have someone so proportionate
that with every twist and turn
my body aches their flesh would soak
and immerse the definition of forever
i would dance willingly without a strain
in the puppeteer's command
my gestures would candidly confess
and not even a stricken match or any other translation of fire
could ever extinguish my feelings for her
my bones made from the trees planted in her yard
and the soils of others tarnished our season of growth
it was supposed to be our year
as we planned years prior our escape from the heckles
and gossips from the bored housewives
that breathe for the burning of our enchanted forest
those long walks underneath rainbows
and dreaming skies
we were young at loves demand and there was nothing
that could fuck up the desire to be together

you questioned my tears
as they slowly crept around the corners
of my insecurities and drained into the bottomless pit of fear
i am so afraid to love her complete
so frightened and apprehensive to give her my wooden heart
she seemed to carry a carving knife in her words
that could chisel my worth into kindle
and her tongue soaking with fuel
can so easily bring me to ash
i've been a keen puppet with vivid eyes
so sharp that wounds expose
and slivers fasten with my glance
but there is no chance to duel
for she is a widow of living men
and knights have crumbled in battles in attempts to love her
i slouch here hoping to understand
as i dangle and sway with every encounter
my love intensifies and deepens with every kiss she allows
i squint my eyes and notice hers are wide open
like she is waiting for my entire breath
to be released so she owns my air
i'm scared of her
i plead to the creator
i ask him to give me strength
to understand her elements of earth...

~ap~

the wonder of you makes me wander...

~ap~

i teeter-totter as u just keep me hanging on
just a breath above water and a contradiction of song
my gills are hooked for the taste of metal
bullets mirage as i love you, but you couldn't ever settle
i choke to evoke what was once broke
to poke and soak from the foolish folk
who never listened just spoke and don't give a fuck if i croak
because they thought i was a joke
this world is all lies
polluted metaphors and other people's smoke
so just please let me write
my eyes are my own sight
i'm not in love with you because i'm married to the night
sodomized labels you shove in me out of spite
like an eagle and a mouse
i'm at a different height
so stop your flight
i'm not writing this for tits and cock
or for minutes of infatuation stock
for my words they are tripping
overload snapshots of my brain to explain
you wouldn't understand you're not my strain
this isn't a game
just a lonely poet stroking his pen
in a self- absorbing gain...

~ap~

true love exists in between
the crevasse of a smirk
so societies remedies are exploited
by the arrogance of a corporate jerk
now the world decided to sneeze back now
from all of you coughing with hands
that feed the instant gratification of how
if government claims to love the voice of all
pushing pens, in judgemental tight suits
in provoking a revolutionary brawl
puffed up lips, pussy softened grips
lost of hope gambling all my chips
mental health pouring out scripts
from my youthful past, psychedelic trips
fear of my own sun
humbled of my own eclipse

sailed into isolation of my lonely ships
fake love is extinct
underneath the fossils of a grin
hoping my greed is hungrier
than your white-collar sin
pushing rocks in attempts
to entertain and win
with no competition
to be more unique in all oceans i swim
i'll tear like a hyena
ripping lies from your pointing limb
i am the baker and the cream i'll skim
in locked jars, fast cars
brother behind bars
no child night light to settle my dim
i win

~ap~

i was once...

you know the journey of an angel
is not quite as luxurious as you might gather
those harsh ruthless storms with wreaking ball swagger
thrusts all fragile innocence
into a squall of unfathomable ache
the softness of each feather soon quivers
with discomfort in an alluring attempt to soar
eyes sting even when closed
to remind oneself of things unseen
when flying above
you witness the incoherent gluttony of the changing world
each leaf silently coughs hiding between a breeze
and a sneeze from a plastic tree
the people down there don't notice me
as i try to stand asserted in my odyssey of night
under the shades of midnight is where i get lost
all the abuse i shoved in holes of misuse for your disposal
landmines they are now and at times erupt
and emit the brokenness of these wings
each angel must learn to fly alone
you have no teacher or mother to guide

just a slow descend into a nest
you built with the person in the mirror
if you stand still for a moment
you can sometimes hear the whisk of others
fluttering on by just waiting for a crash
and they hurry back to their branches
to beak and cackle
i know they do this, you know why
because before i was an angel, i was a crow
my dark endless black pelt was just like yours now
so i don't judge you
i know who you are because i was once you
i now can't live without the dream
and all the ways to get to it
feather by feather i flock with eyes
as windows and a poet with oceans of ink
there is one thing that you must learn
you can never hold time by holding time still
like the agony from a promised kiss
or the dying thirst for pain again
let me go so i can grow a new set

~*ap*~

quarantine

the sick world just told me that i was ill like you
and not the colour of my face or cross-bearing shoulders
could make me believe it's not true
as the wrinkles deepen
time is like the friend who left town
so my loneliness keeps seeping
i somehow glare at my grin
in hopes i find that little person that hides within
hide and seek was a child's game
but it has been just a different type of same
i still wake up young at my mind's doorstep
knocking on windows to play
with love once pure...
a lemon slice, your first morning tear
your second orgasm, hands on my hips
you pushed me at bay
a hungry tongue coiled with a promise of a fable

i was always in love with art
and you were that
so my eyes were forever able
how i think back just a few layers down
a soup ladle i scooped i prevented your hunger to drown
i told you to believe and just hold on to my star
we closed with eyes wide open
and hidden under each other's scars
you told me you were afraid of forever
the part where it eventually ends
so i left and burned a twin flame in lost friends
i now will go back to cutting my own wrists
to expose my ink clean
in my world this poet can't die
in a heartache, in a desert
and in the blackness or a quarantine

~ap~

april fool

we were lost but emerged from dried soil
thirsty as a butterfly's tongue
and winks from glass to sun
inside february's frost
the corners of your forgotten eyes buried our truth
as march took us towards
the promenade of our future parade
with a slight touch of your shoulder
i was undone by the gentle churn of your smoulder
my lasting embers cried like fractured amber
and i saw my breath taper into two
my now sorrow soaked pillow
and the old boyfriend shirt
is put away to close you
for my inexhaustible failure at showing you
i strove to forget the colour of your blue
all the hundreds of dawns i've wasted
every hour you gave up
there follows an endless cruelty
that minutes freeze

it wears me out
that our plans are sewn shut
by strings as thin as web
but as sticky as lust's stains on my grip
last night i slept
eyes shut with a burning mind
like a spitting fuse of dynamite
only fumes in my empty heart smooth
around echoes that tell me i need you
if my mother was alive
she would tell you that i really love you
she would say sorry and apologize
for never teaching me how to hold you
she would say it would be a mistake to give up on me
a block away tossing fate so cruel
you'll never find someone
who loved you as much as i did
he's just a lost aprils fool

~ap~

i even miss u
when i'm with u...

~ap~

detached when thought matched
polished but inside scratched

~ap~

the overrated poet

in the wait always late intoxicated state feels great
is it cause i'm lugging hate or i have no fate?
i don't feel too good must have been something i ate
i look in the mirror and i rate
then look down at the numbers of my weight
for the fake fucking world that i create
just want to lose 5, 6, 7 or eight
i hope i fit into this outfit so i can impress my date
so i'll suppress the gay and pretend i'm straight
for my hypothesis and opinions have such a shallow debate
so i'll live alone and not enjoy you, i'll just masturbate
holy fuck i'm overwhelmed there's too much on my plate
i don't feel like even working to pay for my estate
so i'll shut down my curtains and fasten my gate
keeping friends and acquaintances at bay

i don't even want to talk to my mate
i'm just babbling on or do you relate?
don't you get it? do i have to translate? or dictate?
all the fish in the sea they say, but i got no bait
so all i'll do is my art and recreate
until my eyes dilate and my brain will inflate
with all my frustrations that make me irate
ok ok i'll smoke one and drink two to sedate
i'll get off my babble and deflate
wakey wakey here's an update
for my last attempt to resonate and irritate
until your opinions don't matter
as you read my poem you will overrate

~ap~

be careful boy
without love you will do
whatever it takes to survive...

~ap~

i love your demons
like the devil only can...

~*ap*~

silence of rain

into the silence of the rain
is where wounds strengthen with every drip
all exits exude secrets and prevent sins from secrecy
and all its promiscuous crave
a plethora of glut swallows convenience
inside a drawer a diamond ring remind
and feed fat your revenge
like a slap on the mouth
you must be certain you'll speak
when you're supposed to listen
words are what cuts
and bleeding is everything i've ever known
while callouses are drawn and that has ever grown
with every breadth of your pass
i collapse in a deficiency of decline
and waiting is like a rapist
who entered my room one last time
to sodomize my wish, in puddles, down your cheek
and all oceans i swim to get away from you
i'm alone now with midnight fucking me
on the floor is where i learn to stand
just a kiss away my howl cries inside your poison
as i motion to the moor
i'm not free from your spell
and the tracks of despair are fastened a bit more
i'm blue...

like a dirty bruise and memories that i don't want to obtain
a million bad dreams are all i'm left with
and i have no choice i must learn to refrain
you took everything when you blew away
all the hues that i ever understood
so i now build walls instead of bridges
from the metal of bullets
instead of the roots and stems of wood
i looked inside your skin underneath a plagiarism of paint
and i saw your true colours only the blind could taste
and tasting i did
there's always going to be a more prettier face
a deeper smile that i couldn't resist or a better lover
with whiter sheets than all the clouds
i've ever dreamt to perch
but i never fell in love with the reflection of my eye
i loved you with eyes closed where only poets survive
on the edges of tongue, on the pulsating wrists
inside fibres of flesh
and on the doorsteps on your black carefully guarded heart
and there i was...
in the dawn of the world's end
i pledge in the pain of this lonely pandemic

~*ap*~

trying to ease

so what now can i reach for
when love has vanished
now i count the ways in pleasures of my pain
my quiet mind quivers
with the drought of my words in a speech full of desires
through windows to mirrors
that allows my sadness to unwind
i confess all struggles that i meant to forget
in all my traceless attempts
i've walked through dreams bigger than walls
and i've asked the lord to soften
the hardness of my shadows
i try to erase...
but the bind of my feelings collect
when agony invited the lost invitations of our last kiss
i melt into tedious temptations
i kindly prepare with honest words
written for your pillow
and the softness of your fallen petals
these words always find hidden wounds

and i strive entirely to convey the secrets of my strength
you have broken my lips
somehow where nothing dwells but love
i arrive at your door to tell you
let's go back to the stars and the beginning of our mistakes
you are my dark and i am your knight
with love sharp as a sword quick to slay
when i kill each hour that you seem to haunt
i am scared of losing the ability to dream
inside the moon's warmth and outside of my cold heart
i can't disguise my bare bones
for the rattles in my memory 3 years deep
you stung me on the way out
where the bottom of my heart still winces for your thorn
if you still reach over the side of your bed to find me
cry again
because if missing you was one word it would read death

~ap~

you pulled on my sweater
on the corner of my neck where you once laid your lips
you found a frail string and you pulled and pulled
when i come undone who can repair me?
i stencilled all the nights on empty canvasses with no paint
the feeling you let fall grew into vines
and my values could never be measured in value
as you ignore my attempts to love you
you try to drown the sun
and in the light's sadness, i see
as embers decide to burn forever
as i fall through shades of shadows
i'm left with the storms to dredge
now time fragile in its falter i clip my own wings
and i lay pressed into the earth
when leaping from clouds i struggle not to look down
on all my regrets that my bones reclaim
to all the songs rewritten for us
in all melodies, the memories of your kiss
cradle my crippled wing
hidden in sharp roses true love dried
like dancing sand falling

from the hands that watered your seed
the stars are in every city
and the moon remembers us watching
as time froze the clock's arms
that are now too long to hold past minutes
one second at a time the pain is let out in dreams
that replace the god's choice
beneath the floods, within the gloom
from darkness to gleam
to a blind friend you assume
time the most precious gift to our world
and subjected to more abuse than any other
now i'll let go not far to keep
because yesterday was something i never thought of keeping
so i'll have to answer to whom gave the colour to the sunset
and now the shadow's purpose
is a sad attempt to shred me apart
for all the symptoms of a cohesive embrace

~ap~

above wings

when you say goodbye to the years and tears
you must swallow in the shallow attempt to sing again
these are the moments that bind
a cold shoulder shrugs that shouldn't have defined us
you know i'm right for you, but we turned left
we denied the most important ingredient
that makes all yesterdays feel like now
love is now...
love is stronger than light
you can close your eyes and be blind and it still finds a way
mixed within tear drops tied together with invisible chains
that lock fasten softly with dreams of making it
defining the odds of everyone's predictions
every time i pick up my pen
the ink bleeds inside words and within wounds
written in these pages are the truths
i've never be able to explain
about the one i lost and continue to lose the same

~ap~

last one...

i should have held your hands in front of other eyes
i should have yelled out you're mine
i should have held you and never let go
but you cannot fuck with time
i should have proven that you were her or him
and stared deeper than my black eyes can dig
every scratch my nails scarred, a testament i couldn't rig
my words were once used to kiss you
in a way my tongue touched your ears
but now tarnished by a plethora of eyes
now shuts all my language of years
you know you can't kill a poet
by spearing his purpose of will
because all pain and loves brokenness
will bleed until my words again spill
i'm left without a name and a face, black and new
to kill this poet once and for all
i'll have to learn to forget about you...

~ap~

my infrastructure is not like before
it's rotting like a worm's home
in soil i haven't experienced crawling through
how this poundage of sadness lures
its confusing smug appetite into a silent seep
diamonds are eyes
and charred shrapnel holds the foundation of my function
everything leaves me dry
sixty percent of my body parched
in a perversion of false synonyms
like the shape of water
you don't know the circle of my self-destructive slaughter
his ideas are a sinner's luxury
as you all watch it grow and fall
the opinions of the opponents
in all opportunity oppose others
to never stop and smell the flowers he grew
in all honesty
these thorns help him from slipping
in and out of love's tangled bind
finding himself
in a field of fatigue
he must get help
to find an ordinary pursuit of chaos

~ap~

a lick of a paintbrush pounded into the desert sand
feather by feather i try to stay blind to the ghosts i withstand
there is no such thing as make-believe
they would try to convince our fears
and only you can save me from myself
which others have tried for years
a fake poet inside a clever dance
with moves only a tongue could jive
you can't hold water with a clenched fist
when you're lent the privilege to be fucking alive

~*ap*~

when you dream there are no lies
like a widow in the dark
with taste in her lips like poisonous bark from trees planted
with dust i stroll on my sore soul
and i became a better climber
i tried to yell to everyone who will listen
and you whisper back my name
i fell in love with the dark in all its suspense
and uncertain pressure
i love how night steals the blue from your eyes
and places it in the right spots of regret
closer to the empty side of my gloom
i try not to remember you
when i undress my own wounds
and cut into a deeper truth inside the despair of light
i am starting to get scared of the seconds of dark
i begin to dread tomorrow
if only it stays shadowed by yesterday
i will try not to forfeit my words
and burn my shield i hold like hands clenched on my face
i thought the grass was greener
while you cut deep in the other sides of pain
he was just money, i was a field of fire

your heart was made of paper, and i was the flame
now i battle the sunshine for tomorrow will be too late
my gills fill with tears
in oceans i cannot find the perfect island that we rested on
with carpenter eyes i was left to finish building next changes
and i cannot hold time by holding wasted seconds
as we wait the rust climbs over the diamond skin
as the memories of decay lost the touch of love
velvet was her hold, as we slept with open eyes
drenched wings was his soul while they both tried to soar
we allowed our senses to love each other
but only if we were held tight no more
as soon we inhaled and i took another breath to live
her heart shot back jagged bullets
to hurt me every time she pulled out
i couldn't make her see anymore
if we didn't make it by now i must try
and figure out how to get through the loss of memories
and to love myself somehow...

~ap~

cat scratch

i've made mistakes so i can learn when fallen
deeper than words dare to write
i guess i was addicted to sadness
and enslaved to chains by madness i fight
how could i lie with my hands
you cannot deny those touches
how could i lie with my eyes
like arms they held you in clutches
the first time the senses adored you
we couldn't resist the sins
my wishes demanded entry to your dreams
despite the vows, storms and grins
we've made mistakes so that they learn when rising
not a fake, a fraud, a follower, i'm not disguising
a tortured boy holding a hand of a hurt girl
whose skies and roads lead us that day

when this knight and queen couldn't destroy
the dragons of love
we allowed hurt victorious to slay
if i had the chance to sail her ocean eyes
just for seconds that's all that is needed
i would toss our seeds into the twin flames
to the bottom of the ocean
where they will be seated
perhaps a fish will prey on them again
and the fish gets captured and put on a plate
until garbage was thrown
as the cat scratched the bag
and buried the loss of fate

~ap~

jerry cordeiro

i fucked with fate and it fucked me back
i kept fucking with it and it scratched until attack
now i find i try to fondle with love again
and all i cum is these words spewed out of my pen
i'm not sure if i'll ever get my lust to befriend my heart
but they say old dogs do learn
and it's never too late to restart
so fuck you to the heckles of others tied in social knots
because...
i am an artist
and you are replaced by the other wind's thoughts...

~ap~

broken leaves

in a fortune teller's eyes
what if i was wrong
when the words have all burnt
i became a lover of light
and friends with the night
my brittle attempts with no value
raise old graves in soil to blame
the sweetest years soured the path of past
only hands clenched in knuckles
bruised in smears of ink
heavy-hearted in a long wail
i hold as i try to prevail
things are kept close
to the holster ready to shoot
emotions overly stack
and the dirty dishes crust in yesterday's hunger
i secure you with strings tied
from a young willow to an old stump
in the death of the flowers
broken leaves lie again in folding seasons
our age will forgive
and i'll make angels sigh
in shattered attempts of pockets with change...

~ap~

we were laying under midnight
the stars tuned sharp in songs we wept
two lost souls where even a preacher could not school
our full-fledged silence continues
to invite my conscious without warning
i was drawn from memories of a sleeping past
where your skin bathed by the morning sun
i could not commit my love to convey
emitting glare that seldom shown
the wind roughing my lonely pelt
and travel remains silted
under the dirty ground and dead leaves
all our insecurities of the audience
fizzed like artificial sweetness
your fragile mind in years fold
while the ocean leaves and returns again
barely even after the pain of battle
i dig trenches to learn from my mistakes at war
now i stagger throughout already brittle leaves
turning wounded reds to the bruises
around my heart as you squeeze
lacerated fingertips lick among drooping tears
salted souls are then torn by streets on a recluse to comfort
i cry out grey and settle for night
i whistle for a bird
but the storm-beaten wings rest forever away
and forever away i shall rest...

~ap~

whatever the odds may be i leap
i leap a stride of fallen leaves before a regretful windy day
these saddened eyes held high
in disguise turned blues to grey
now i'm more inclined to tears i see such verse
nature took breath to dance along the leaves
ruthless gestures left unborn
lovingness that carried some sight
held by some dream beside the frail me
my fallen shade slips
lift me with gentle threads held tight and secure
i bear my scars to the constant stars
where permanent shadows lengthen into dark
accept love like an all-consuming fire
i rest patiently until shine replaces last remnants
eyes that say what yesterday denied
love again persuades the air with no erased sounds
where dark is upon a fading sky and the hills unhurt by war
soothe with vague plateaus i crawl
every restless thought is burnt three layers deep
into an aching heart you arrive and stay
to meet you at the edge of the ocean shore
for the last feelings that i inhaled of you
i should have never let go

~ap~

lips of converse

what can i reach for when love has vanished
let me count the ways in pleasures of my pain
my quiet needs a speech full of desires
through windows to mirrors that allow sadness to unwind
i confess all struggles that i meant to forget
in traceless attempts
lord has softened the hardness of shadows
to brighten my midnight and lead me to dawn
sunflowers searching directions
and extracting polluted breath
bind my feelings collected
when agony invited with lost invitations
envelopes sealed sailing to places i've wished to sea
my weak wings flap in treading skies
where storms await placid havens

i melt into tedious temptations
kindly prepared with honest loafers
silver spoons and thorns in pillows
you fool not only your steps when halted
the love i had was selfless and faulted
fading stars slip and i continue to wonder
i pulled in when your mind goes
as i release others and collect all concerns
my devotion forms pictures re-enacted and positioned
float in vulnerable flees one city at a time
these winds always find hidden wounds
as i peel bandages helicoptered into discipline
i ask myself should i strive entirely to convey
all my secrets that strengthen in lips of converse...

~*ap*~

that i see

you ruin me from the inside like a villain or a thirsty kitten
tongue like shards of glass tossed at sea
i am sorry i never made it better
we pulled each other off of shoulders of our fears
that i can no longer rest my head on again
i knew you weren't convinced
but i didn't give it all
i would have broken my heart clean in half
if only you gave your peace as well
i am the one that would have ruined your lipstick
tasting like it was your first kiss all over and over again
we would have lived forever
or discovered something in us that would
those dying embers will soon waft
with perfumes of my red scarf
when inhaled they heave those knees to fall
wasn't it beautiful when you believed in everything
our plans, our vision, our laying under white sheets

you will now forge from ocean to roads hunting for a knight
already dreamed of a thousand midnight sleeps
my soul was no place for a little girl
but a woman with chaos in her screams
and adventure in her veins
the only thing now that is real is that everything i do
you'll be alive forever
in my dead attempts
with dead flowers in my books
in my alive hands that hold tightly
on every shooting star that i see
because i am the poet
and words are what feeds me

~*ap*~

everything to everyone

it seems you have me exactly where you want me
on a glass island surrounded by rocks
where no one can love me like you left me time inside time
you tossed me like i was through
like i was empty, like i wasn't brand new to you
the mistake was yours
if only you wanted to see those dreamy nights inside oceans
and skies not wanting anyone to save us
we were everything that books and poets bleed from
a knife for a pen and a life to share amongst two hearts
but again your sail was taken by pirates
new friends with patches for eyes
didn't see the beauty
when you were only a belief from crying alone
i was everything to you, but they are now
with touches of gold all treasures of me get buried
three years deep under a lifeless sea
everything to everyone except me...

~ap~

i love you more than paper and paint
more than scratches on a mirror
or burning sage in my hand
you were my paper
and i was the flame
i wanted all of your ashes
but your yearn
just wasn't the same...

~ap~

bullet

he falls every day through my time-worn fingertips
with only fear clenched in my grip
now i can't look at anyone else
because it is not him leading my script
his face sculpted with sins of love's mistakes etched
from ruptured teachings from his peers
that lost, forgotten once innocent child was buried
with neglect and misplaced years
i writhe and coil beneath
my eyes like glass, precipitate as i jar
i'm a fugitive to the felony of poems
because the pain of words spell out my scars
his hands poetize the tame of his lion's zeal
a desire for an endeavor of lust
i could feel his strength on the edge of softness
the slivers of my bones he needed
and the anguish of my thrust
those rusted lips of his withered with lies
and bitten from other teeth of grins

how can you blame the innocence of a child
with no consciousness of his sins
his heart is left for only guesses to say
i would have tried endlessly to change him to a proper way
he camouflaged his sensibilities for his own fear of loves kill
what a lonely existence he must swim
in shark waters with a seized pair of gills
in his eyes disguised as diamonds of hurtful words
and sticks and stones
if i do forever lose him i'll spiral
not in circles but like a landslide of the unknown
he says i love you so fluently
like a spit from a striking dalliance snake
if i do lose him forever i will never know
if the love that poisoned my heart in two
was a bullet or a fake

~*ap*~

cry baby cry

as i dry not wanting us to die

from the holes of a lie and the excruciating fry

when i get down from this high

it will be her turn to weep to the heavens and ask why

she hesitated and i knew the answers why

her broken dishes

my cry

this is why she didn't try

i wasn't that guy

as i bite my tongue and i sigh

all these questions and answers i pry

the only thing i am going to miss

is her hold and kisses on the thigh

i guess i just ain't that guy

i was gas on fire to apply

on her leaves of fakes trees up high

don't pretend that you're shy

or add colour to my character to dye
all i wanted was the recipe of your pie
and to be the only guy
like the ones that live forever
like knights in a lullaby
so purchase a new friend
and whatever you can buy
cause on my own opportunities is where i lie
on gypsy skin she won't deny
cause for someone else i will be their treasured guy

~ap~

jerry cordeiro

eyes...

i confess
i miss you
i confide
i need you
i enclose
i cry for you
i contain
i still love you
i release
i hate you
i learnt
i hurt myself
i recognize
i lost you
i allowed
i got fooled by you
i decided
i must let go

~ap~

i knew she didn't truly love me
simply by the way she loved me...

~*ap*~

it was a great mistake
our kiss met and forever i will regret
with a pair of wings i would tell the stars that i miss you
while i'm up there i would gather about a thousand dreams
that i wouldn't change
i can't understand why it didn't work
i instinctively know every crevice
every imperfection, every crack on that concrete heart
the same ones you would step on
to break my back and not avoid
i've waited my whole life for someone like you, or i thought
the dead roses chipped with time eventually get tossed
and new flowers will blossom
the book you gave me still firm in anticipating my return
another time? another place?
these tracks seem to go forever
and your train never arrives to carry me
did you fool me with your tongue?
those words along with your juice knew where i needed relief
fill my bucket you would say, as you kicked mine over
spilling fears of all your exes that marked your spots
i don't admire this hurt inside my brand new breath
where kisses from your mouth make broken look beautiful
it's easy on my mind to allow your memory to nestle in place
you were there in death, you were there in passion

but you left when needed
i will not forget how easy it was for you to walk away
your knees must have healed
by the eager prance you vanished
in this world where everyone is plastic
you seem to be wanting the synthetic way
this wild man will learn to fly
without planes, without cars, without you and your scars
this i will know, that the memories will remain
and what only the day brings i'll devour and gain
i lost you once before but this time i found who you truly are
you would have settled me if you waited a bit more
but i bit more than you could chew
i saw the frightened girl in her purist form
i let you be you, completely and incomplete
i allowed you to cry as i tasted those tears
to make sure it wasn't a mirage
but now i feel dim, like a fridge light, closed and cold
only until you want a piece
your lazy feeling will haunt you
like a ghost they appear in the corners of your thoughts
they will repeat, i wonder if i ever loved him?
beneath me and over my skin, i build a castle
of all the sand crushed by the rocks you threw

~ap~

today it stopped, today i began
i'm smashing my fists, dismantling her shrine
wrenching her flesh between her heart and mine
the letters i have given or the poems that spew
will burn like sage getting her curse out of view
the smell of her pillow, the taste of my fingers after a gush
if others only knew the secrets of her hush
no more afflictions of all the webs your thoughts spun
because today it stopped, today i begun
a winter of unforgettable cold
i mean your heart, your words, and the lies you hold
spring will do exactly that
my flower will sprout
the air will bring transparency to my onward jaunt
killing the ghosts of 1095 days of you
i will never let you haunt

the tall grass we once dreamed beneath will be for a new rest
you can try and hurt me with your slander
but karma will be your next guest
i'm left now again and again and again forevermore
these words i bleed are not for you, but me evermore
the café was quiet, not a whistle from a mouse
so was the lonely last drive on the dirt road from your house
there was not a single tear that let the mirror heed
the forfeit of a carpenter's daughter
she built to destroy with nails dug in greed
i sat smashing my wits
constructing my wings in famine for her
i left not to ever return
and this last poem is my cure...

~*ap*~

jerry cordeiro

the sad cafe...

bludgeoned until my heart aches differently
each time your words strike i plummet all the way back
just a sliver farther than my attempts to change
little pinpricks lifting my wounds
stick in my confusion of your purpose
you say goodbye like a murderer
your knife dull rusted
and stained from your previous heave
your agony like a revolver
your torture aims like scorching bullets
searing all those vital echoes of magic
the laceration of my love will last longer
then the longing i had for you
i guess i flew too close to your frayed lines

where monsoons of songs i'm reminded
now the calmness arrives, and i fly
will you regret this if either of us died?
will you regret to learn how it felt the seconds i entered?
i have stopped dying for you
and death like wine will stain a mother's child
a plethora of ambitions would have held you
for the rest of your life
serendipity now is wounded at war
the battle now will only be our unknown
the calmness arrives
and i fly to the beginning of the sad cafe

~*ap*~

shining torture

i understand that love has different stages
this is mine today...
carried on a perpetual feud
upon my shoulders such outward signs of love appear
where things altogether fell beyond my reach
i stood where i was left, towards the end of a persistent cry
you don't hear me wail
you can't feel me squirm
but you will remember me
i'll be in that dream when you least expect it
walking carelessly without questions or answers
my scent will then follow and you'll feel it
our future world which held the promises
has been punctured
and i'm spinning out of control
inside nights, it will be hard
the anguished thump of my black heart
will want the feel of flesh
not soft, but the burn from my nails
as i tear to introduce your wounds
i can't extinguish it
i can't burn it to ashes because ashes are easily swept
and blown where dust is ruthlessly waiting
to kill the love story

was it fake?
were the gypsy tellers fucking with us
when they said this is real
or does fate insinuate hate on loves gate
in all the disastrous wars we stand to free the slaves
but serve the promise to endure the fight
i am tired, i am fearless, but i'm afraid of never trying
i will fall
but i will crawl
and when i'm that low to the ground
i become accustomed to the bruises on my knees
i would have walked a thousand miles
with irresistible wonder
could you have been all i ever needed?
i find a hole where all those tears fell into it
and i quench the thirst
i squish it all till it hurts
i forage like a wild horse looking for rest
i've got less time to soar and more places to fall
so fuck all the ways of love
i will slaughter that feeling if it ever comes close again
like a knight of shining torture

~*ap*~

if this is goodbye...

under ice i melt
and the fire i once had flickers until my blinks finally die
if this is goodbye you must know that i loved you
even when my tongue coiled like a striking snake
venom from my sorrow
and the poison from the drips i sucked between your legs
i'll crave tomorrow
all those delicate words you stowed inward
have become clear
how could he say these things to me you ask?
how could she lie to me, i grasp
you were the one that made me feel like i could be me
and now, i'm left choking my own doubt
with hands tattooed forever
if this is the end i'll have to find why my skin burns
when i think of you
is it because you were fire or were you a razor
and you cut little slits that i couldn't bandage
at one time you use to fit so perfect inside my curled-up body
i would ever so gently feather my fingers on your side
writing love stories on your body of mine
how we would kiss, it felt like it was exactly how it should be
gentle at first, fierce, dangerous

and times cruel, to which blood
and pain would romantically fuse
i would give so much to sit across from you again
watching people look at us
as though we are the translation of love
it's true, we had something
it's true we didn't know how real it was
i will search in my heart in vain
and realize i hurt you because of my own pain
inside a breathless suspense i'll try not to run into you
while i'm chasing clouds
and searching for something a little like you
our rare love was eventually extinct
from the poachers you invited to love what was only mine
now you will never know or find someone like my kind
so enjoy them for now
but remember plastic people can't dissolve into beauty
they fill the land where rubbish gets forgotten
i made my love cry
and vanish for the last time so i could trust again
our famous last words weren't beautiful chords
sang from our heartstrings
they were caged birds that wept in secrets
if this is goodbye
i will not show up at your door with lost shoes
i will find my lost soul somewhere far from yesterday...

~ap~

bad dream...

i had a bad dream inside my sleeps you were gone i knew exactly the reasons but i couldn't hold on i thought about blaming my childhood and the places i didn't belong so here goes the nightmare and my familiar song like an antique i critique all the tryings to reach my peak with a tarnished reputation streak of a sneak weak freak ill adore kicking asses all week just for you to speak and tweak off your entitled beak i don't fucking care about your opinion if you're western virginian or you got a flat tire on my dirt road and wreaked your rack and pinion for a fake lending hand over absolute dominion i'll settle quite slowly with the noose a little loose wrapped around the neck of my honest truth you surrender and call truce for your own use to squeeze dollar bills juice now there's no need for your nectars soft drip abuse i've mention a million times there's no one like me mate and i won't fall for that bait and hate don't try to imitate this fucken kid been eating staring contests since he's been eight so there's no debate i'll tell you straight i don't support your state so open your gate and let me create so you again will have to wait to castrate my artistry's debate where every eye that you donate like a dealer with a machine gun

i checkmate i will frustrate and fixate i'm no light-weight
for critics to mandate with my own voice i will narrate my
own primate i will never need to update so don't waste your
hate just acclimate i gave myself to the earth and requested
your apple seed with every month promise in all lovers
greed i made it clear that i need i thought you agreed to lead
instead you lead me to the stampede i couldn't succeed so
i had to proceed a falling father a death by a mother from
falling in lies all seams were never sewing ignoring loud
whispers blowing of all secrets that love was never knowing
slap this pen from my hands and strain the ink dry for all i
have left is a thousand letters inside my cry for this bad guy
who was actually shy two pinches of high with the black
eye and a poet's comply that could never deny you lost me
and i just your ghosts exist that i'll try to shoo how lonely
now the sky in its faded blue as stars mock me still leaving
no sudden clue throughout the caged innocent zoo that we
both threw it was just us two and you knew oh baby blue

~*ap*~

in-between nothing and zero
i broke my own heart to save my soul
i let him go, to keep myself from falling
if it was ever meant to be
then i guess it will find its own way
but my heart has no place for fear
just every idea of what love actually felt like
it is not you that i can't get over
it's the deep cuts
deeper than blood
and farther than never again...

~ap~

i came rushing in like a thief stealing stars
or a bear with his claws inside honey
i tore a bit of flesh on my way in
and ripped the thin wall of silence
you were shocked, not by my rage in my eyes
but by the amount of moisture your dry soul had buried
i want to make you believe in me cause my belief is brief
your paper heart will continue to be written on
with words that lick stamps sent to find you
i hold you close, too far to keep
too far to let in, but close enough to taste
i look up at you
and i watch your grimacing face
wanting to choke all my words
but i'm used to that grip
i've fallen in love with the closeness of death...

~ap~

toss me in a wishing well

our tangled bine somehow has a way
there's midnight in her eyes as mornings gallop in the real
i'll fall into your dream
and make sure that all my thoughts of you are long
so long, as men could breathe
like a searching heart but soon it turns to ghosts
as regretting instead of forgetting lingers
i wonder
your poignant gestures have wakened all my fears
visiting my spaces with sticky gears
our ravished attempts to understand
through rutted trails muddy and clear
a house without comfort can only continue to break
into shards of glass gleaming with escape
can't get you out of my mind
and i can't get you into my heart
i can't hold you close because i don't have you near
and i can't stop loving you even when i try
so please stop pushing
and i'll try to stop pulling
you tossed me in a wishing well
and i lost you the same way
just one last time please touch my mouth
or i'll be the widow of your kisses no more

~ap~

on the path of loneliness

our push has stopped
and the wind is tired of trying
so much wasted moments
in vanity has now vanished like magic
this is what you get
you'll get exactly what you wished for
when you toss so many changes in my well-being
the bitterness is disguised by smiles
but your skin will continue to burn in remnants of my heat
farewell to the songs, goodbye to the notes
these dreams of mine will cause storms
and everyone will hear my thunder, except you
i dwell in my discomfort so don't worry about me
my country eyes and your city lips will only speak in urge
you won't get sympathy from my tears
they are made out of clay
i will then mold my own cries for things i can actually hold
change is like a fold on a creased blanket
you forget the smell and you forget the feel
if the sun refused to be kind to me
then i will fuck the night and make it bring me all yesterdays
because yesterday was mine and i will not give it back

~*ap*~

i lay her down just far enough for my hands to detain
if she squirms to release
i glare through her thoughts and survey her skin
her bottom lips give off this heat that i can feel with my taste
i swallow hard so she knows exactly what i thirst for
she sighs, arching her back
letting her petals fill with more moisture
between her tight jeans
and the fibres from her damp seams
i move in, like the silence from a cheetah
on the tips of a pounce
i expose my nails pressing her wrists
farther in the pillow-like clay
i move in
i give her my entire tongue as deep as i can stifle
her fear climbs inside my body
as i try to asphyxiate her arousal
i let go, i let go to let her breathe
she knows by now i am not a fucking parody
she removes her pants quickly with conceit
in her attempts to gain control
i slam her arms down again
making her repeat my lustful threat, "stay the fuck down"
a last breath
i slither my days unkept whiskers
and i move all the way down to her feet
along her knees piercing the parade of goosebumps
like a menace with pins in a room full of balloons
there is only one spot i need to ravage

i slowly snake closer with eyes squinting
in anticipation for a kill
i can smell her already, the day's movements
the hours left constrained and the minutes before my visit
i close my eyes to complete my attack
i gently remove my grips from her hands nailed firm
and i slightly ever so tranquil
push the thin soaked material to the side
her lips open and fold to the invitation of my kiss
i attack
i bury my mouth into her roots, below flesh
and all the distances i journey
i suck her relentlessly like it's a pomegranate seed
i swirl all edges forging for more rain
those open window blinds i cradle with my teeth
i look up at her, pulling my head back
and watching her quiver back into form
a moan from a distance i ignored
the instincts made her hands leap
pressing my head farther and deeper inside her well
now her control is mine
with slender fingers she flutters with years of rhythm
i slurp, i absorb, i regurgitate, i inhale
i wash down the juice, as i come to the point of feeding her
and all of a sudden i wake up
treading in my own wet dream

~ap~

jerry cordeiro

i couldn't take all the promises that you make
for the empty words that i've learnt was fake
you were like a drug that i couldn't put down
like the sway of a forgotten leaf
eventually hitting the ground
in my veins you consumed, as i prepared my heart to ruin
just one more hit of your potent inside drip
for only my agony of losing you i constantly slip
punctured with my guilt, with lies of deceitful silt
i can only try and quit your urge
for the love you tease my addiction i must not splurge
i will forever be held by the drug you sold
cause i never knew the effect of love and its crippling hold...

~ap~

i had your word
bandaged my heart with a song
allow all clouds to imitate my imitation of love
i was descending
and my doors are fastened shut now
i'll let no one in
i'll keep all curtains shut
with a tiny pinprick to peek
there will be no tomorrows
just yesterday's glint will be my companion
i will answer my own questions and ask what i know
i will be kind, mindful
and i will share my air
i will give all my attention to my mind
for it has its own way of thinking
at night it will be hard
that black anguished heart still has a flicker
i can't extinguish it
i cannot burn it to ashes
i must just understand
that there is a place in my heart
where you just fell apart
and the bruises that are left
are not from your tongue
but from the lashes of your words

~*ap*~

you were my water...

when my seeds needed to break open

when my leaves were withered with worry

you were my water...

when my thirst for love was parched and brittle

and the cracks inside my heart screamed for your pressed lips

you were my tears...

when i lost you in the lonely rain

and i couldn't tell the difference

between being sad and drowning

you are now a teardrop...

i must wipe off my face

and head straight into the storm

where i feel comfortable dancing with the winds...

~ap~

april's promises

to gaze at length where my blind lonely shoes forgot
hands become conscious of every stone that was thrown
forever faithful to the one adored
and to the bird who you can never change
with love sharp as a sword quick to slay
severed locks helped myself untangle the rips
through sunshine spills and dirty water gills
rain like jewels wear like precious tears
and with vivid past a new day dawns
there is no element ended by reassuring
my inexhaustible energies for us
i strove to forget the laughter that we scattered
the lost keys and the severed locks remain broken

~ap~

fold the tired day like hands in prayer
of desires i cling one moment back
as a sun sends no shadows
my screaming wings upheld above places where i dwell
and now by the force of my own gust of songs
i sang absent in autumn
by now my heart remembers what a smile did
but words that awakened clench like a fistful of fears
what becomes of my broken heart?

~ap~

april's promises

i stopped crying to see clearly
the image of you was upside down inside the drops
inside the tears were artificially synthetic love
like table salt and cheap-ass flowers
that came free with a purchase of lemons...

~*ap*~

let this be the place i die
where birds lost all the songs of morning
and butterflies gave up on the journey to land
on edges of fingertips and wilted petals
the wind somehow makes me question
i gently breathe in and wonder injects me
does he love me better than i can?
could she better me if i could love?
we stretched for all letters that explained
i was relentless in the pursuit to have us breathe together
so eagerly to finally touch air
so all the following whispers will be introduced in red
red is the colour of blood
and words cut deeper than the exposure of wounds
i now fly without purpose
still enduring and with slight realization
love was the easiest part to kill

~ap~

with idle hands
the devil is busy
trying to convince
me to touch
how did he know
i loved the feeling
of scratches

~*ap*~

words are free
all you do is put them
in front of each other
to antagonize each letter

~ap~

continual continuing sprained eager chicken wing
soft tailed pillowed smirk
high levelled charmed the corporate jerk
naive provided, chaperoned guided
my lies subsided, pharmaceutical supplied it
the thrower in the whiskey, the rye in the catcher
media's smorg feared parent child snatcher
seasons fold, two-sided notes, signs, questions, lies
fate remains the only vote
people's care levels, influenced devils
dreams to understand, decorative fakeness, elastic bands
close to death, the breath of sleep
your careless ignorance i will soon defeat
unrecognizably sickened, synthetically engineered, stagnant
unlock pores, empty hallways heap
styrofoam cup holders neck deep
but critically acclaimed ignorance
plastic hours, sweet regrettable pencils
frequently written to poison, dripping purity inside
unnatural fossils that tear
painless pain closer to the bone the undertone
the inability to capture wind or hold onto soul
my hand deep in a dark hole
when i am reaching please console
my mind paints again, brushing questions accordingly
exposing the pain of my intelligence

~ap~

fade into smoke
i will pick through the wreckage
and build my own broken man
to something that someone will know its beauty
when hope died like crumbling wildflowers
you picked from my trail
the pain of each piece dusted into my memories weep
i clench my teeth to halter those tears
in anguished thistles caught beneath you still
only time has left
your burning skin will singe each second
inside the imitate hold of my hand's journey
i fucken promise you, you won't forget me
i will stretch the agony till your breath can only say my name
if you chose to leave
your mind will let you
but your heart on my hand will be squeezed
i kneel on my simplest words
as you lie quietly at your ease
i have no skill to shape unless you mold me to believe
i am only left
with the fragrances that soon fade into smoke

~ap~

treeless yard

the bullets are disguised as feathers
as they fall from a bird without purpose
the butterflies try and open windows
but the flickering of their own reflection confuses the flight
the birds knew how in love it was
but leaves never grew
my wings are without strength
like a nest without warmth
and trees with only branches
the sin of the gun was made from its wood
and as i rifle my words on the paper like skin
it burns to fuck the death of purity
your mind, towards me it pushes off the agony of my sap
that sticky fidget
your hands will not know what to do
with the lack of hanging off my branch
you will weaken till it snaps in two
everything and all
the cradle will fall
and i plant firm and certain

~ap~

oh lord how we slandered

those lies were in your disguise

and i realize it must have been my demise

our plans and a thousand tries

the listening ears of morning cries

it will worsen when he leaves and flies

those dark endless gypsy eyes

will escape societies hold and ties

i've warned you love, it was no surprise

a gemini's gift was not your winning prize

i would have loved you forever with no explanation for size

no heaven could take her unpredictable highs

a simple toss of an unwanted stone in a fake pond of spies

oh lord how we slandered our love, it was not wise...

~ap~

ashes to ashes
dust to rust
what was only burned
was the ability to trust...

~*ap*~

life is just too short to live only for you...

~ap~

april's promises

dreams

i hate you but i love you
i wonder why you made me wait
for an imaginary line called time
i was ready
you will now wait forever
for those circles i drew on your skin
my hands are like no other
my lips chipped by the nine lives i've bitten
all i ever did was wait
seconds, hours, days, years
fate, magic, lust and tears
i'm stuck today in this room
with only you as the window
i stumbled, i fell, i lost
windows pain allows my sky to gain
goodbye smells
goodbye skin that melted into mine
goodbye plans
hello to the old mind that will regret waiting
i will miss the potential
i will miss everything but who you became
i hate to love you
i love to hate you...

~*ap*~

jerry cordeiro

yesterday was something
i never thought of keeping

~*ap*~

our famous last words
are still lying under my tongue
with only kisses between a movie
and heartbreaking songs
the fizz of demise
a soul mate that prematurely
was mistaken and gone
i still need him
like rage needs the seethe of boiling water
and my fury needs my grimacing teeth of wrong
if this is goodbye
then bye, don't prolong
he was my lover
he was my friend
he was my partner
he was my broken soldier
that fought with me all along
but now
his words are lacerating bullets
that claw until i don't belong

~ap~

jerry cordeiro

admiring can hurt in a brand-new breath
where kisses from your mouth
make broken look beautiful
with a pair of wings
i will look for answers in the stars
behind each glimmer
your shadow compromises my walk
up here in this lonely sky
there are about a thousand tiny dreams
i left for you that i wouldn't change
friend of mine, why couldn't you spare
your glass worn shoes forbidden to be us
and dance with dark unaware
old roses chipped with time
and all the things you did brittle to my touch
our dust tangled between a paper palace
where my words seem to seep my wrath

as my pen fucks the paper like an animal in flesh
if only i had won what i've lost over and over
waiting for my luck like a child in the forest
looking for a clover
another time perhaps, another mistake perhaps
your distant sound no longer sings our tunes
your roots and thorns have stopped the ability to consume
so now you have placed me with all emptiness
and ignorance as i fall to catch last tears
that disappear as quickly as dreams
change is found under my deep stitched soul
like slippery eyes, i slip out of control
now i have less time to soar and more places to fall
and your love will be painted more soft as it descends

~ap~

jerry cordeiro

i wonder if we ever think of each other at the same time...

~ap~

a moment late

how life led me
you fell into it where hearts get second chances
and a stolen page from a storybook
with white picket fences
and a trail to taste your flowers
i arrive a moment late to forget your petals
a smile upon my glace and it was enough for sure
all pleasures i've forged in a lonely devour to picture you
there is much grace in the way dreams wake us up
with little thoughts when you shouldn't
no use to destroy what i don't want to fix
so cover me with blankets of clouds
as i continue to pass through
on your borrowed shoulders
where everyone uses to tear on

~ap~

she was like a sunset
beautiful to gaze at and dream
but just like that... she was gone
she will never come back
the same as yesterday promised

~ap~

i would give anything for a day
with the person you used to be...

~*ap*~

she was my simple dream
being us in this world of certain
we planned our escape
when together we could lay under tall grass
and the rest of life would be all we needed...

~*ap*~

i can't forget to remember her gush
what fell into wishing wells, a wish of rush
i used to wash her skin in the shower
with only my hands as stones
i'd slowly drop to my rug burned knees
and meet her lips like a thirsty traveller at a water fountain
at first quench you can't taste what i mean
so i'd scrape with nails exposed
knead my mouth inside, so my tongue belongs to her
it always has
i hold my breath until panic arouses me
i try to drown all possibilities she will never forget me
not the way i fuck, but how hungry my eyes need...

~ap~

jerry cordeiro

are you warm tonight
i can't bear to imagine those goosebumps
on your neck being lonely
i feel i've loved you even before i met you
in a raging pursuit my hands begin to strengthen
i would squeeze until i only can give breath back
i have romanticized death and found a beauty of losing you
but in certain i would have you forever
in between dreams and underneath my skin
my shoulders are carved by tears
i will carry those drops until they melt and seep deep
sky inhales every passing soul
and we would never be alone
i am him
you know that by the way it hurts...

~ap~

faith looks up
so i open my tired eyes
and took the plunge i would love to stay
tasting mornings and playing out between chaos
and light tickles on the side of your ribs
no diamonds and pearls could compete with scratches
beneath desires you continue to enjoy
no one else...
how many times do i have to fucken repeat
angered but horny eyes
strong hands recoil
with teeth grinding discipline to a killers discrete
silent stories which every whisper cries
to allow flowers to guess the drought
in fallen petals your attempt to make me stop will die
beyond a familiar tomorrow we will proceed as planned
for seconds that demand
clenched tight in my secure strong hand
i stare at the innocence inside the screams
pillow thoughts, stomach knots
i fall again in wishes of self-molding dreams

~*ap*~

if only there was a switch
we sang songs together
we cried for each other's loneliness of childhood
we told each other that we cannot break the bond
even if the glass shattered and the shards were sharp
there was nothing we couldn't handle
bleeding wound
hearts that assume
last drop of your perfume
my painful sleeps how they consume
those lies you told they fume
but those plans we had will always loom
is there any wonder i'll wreak
i loved putting my hands around your neck
for days
months
years
i'd trek
to have last nights
to have yesterdays
to kill today
i can't turn you off...

~ap~

we were supposed to show them, but you refused
that despite the other fucks we were solid and fused
but fearful and confused
from our old life that was abused
the little girl's secrets to the permanent scratches
and arms now bruised
we slandered the wish and granted was misused
now we hate from screens and search for the accused
i knew you would let go i'm not that amused
only now you're a someone
that drowned, that forgot, that used...

~ap~

i'm tangled and i sit firm
on the steps of your door i squirm to be let in
just like the stripes of a zebra
i'm confident of my instincts
if you were a fallen flower, i'd put you in my pocket
and keep my hands inside, feeling for a change
if you were a wounded bird
i could take you out of your cage
and ruffle those feathers
strengthen those wings for you
to not fall short of your flight
in my time of dying
you will be the last thought i'd love to smell
my failures sharpen as they leave
cutting deep is the only way to know we are true
they say you don't really change your stripes
but who are they to see your range despite
towards the innocence of love i cowardly constraint
my grip is weak but my desire leaps

and tears you up like a lion on flesh
now comes the time where seconds are heavier
and all your sleeps become windows
those windows are the dreams
you will wish a hundred more times
to find the differences between wind
and the breeze and to avoid the plastic fed trees
what could i offer you in worthy of your veins
now and tomorrow and all the senseless games
i tried to say goodbye to love a thousand times before
but my earth requested
and the universe understood
the importance of a heart to adore
my tears will continue to build roads in a landslide i slip
in sand i allow you to build castles of love letters
and again, it strengthened my grip
i'm tangled, and i stand firm...

~*ap*~

pick up that heart that fell on the ground
so i can fall myself before i drag you through my sound
i've decided to drown out in attempts to slip within
within the places where i thought
you would fit ever so perfectly
why do i always take this lonely road
where i spin and flutter like a butterfly without purpose
i wonder who will love you if our time has broken arms
and seconds burn like thorns in my insides
this is no place for lovers
but sins that singed from fires lost at sea
the things you want i wanted to give to you
listen closely as my eyes shut tight
and i'll stop breathing just to hear you speak
to feel your dreams i allow them to become mine
what if your life stays the same

and you will never know you needed my love
do you pass it by or fall all the way down
my love will never die
it will be buried alive
and will surface when you need it
the moment when you can feel that pain of losing me
is the second you will understand that love was true
if i take your breath away
i will give you mine
i have been holding on to other wings getting mine strong
steady to soar places we close our eyes to
so pick up that heart and place it back in that box
and throw the fucken key as far as we could dream to be...

~ap~

i couldn't unlove her
so i wish i had a river to float away
i wish i could teach my feet to stop falling
for you shallow and deep
when the moon is the only thing that shines
i frantically beg for your gleam
i fall off wild horses cause i'm not used to running free
i blame it on falling stars
they always appear when i wish for you
signs all around and coincidences are too frequent to ignore
it's the smell of your neck
it's that feeling of velvet when i gently slide my fingers inside
it's that snarl
how can i explain to you what my body wants
when i don't understand that desires stranglehold
what makes me feel this way
it's all of you
not only the sweet but that sour taste i grind for
i would walk for days through fields of nowhere
if one chance was left on my windows pane...

~ap~

a million reasons why we shouldn't
no reasons why we couldn't
but only one reason to let go
i looked up at the stars last night
the same ones your sigh and my whisper kissed
i asked them why you denied my try
and without further hesitation
the certainty of love fell into the big dipper
and the clear night clouded
with the walls of my eyes
and i fastened shut
letting go...

~*ap*~

i am a wolf
i was your sheep
i was fooled by your eyes that preyed for my weep
i was a clench that your fangs protrude
you were my health but spit up and chewed
we were the grass in fields of wishes
and you were the net stealing all the rivers fishes
i was the stars that led blind in skies
and i was a fool with rain tangled cries
i needed your hands, kisses and scratches
and you needed my caged soul with feather latches
i loved you like blood introduces the red
and i love you still even though our hearts are dead
i was the one writing words from our love
and you were the accuser denying me
and looking from above
we were a puzzle, broken pieces that fit in place
we will find others, but with a false certain embrace
i am a poet, you can't destroy my tongue
you will fucken regret forever how you tossed and flung
this is the last poem i will ever write for you
because you know how much you killed me
and continue to do
i am a wolf and i will kill the sheep
i have awoken
and your memory is now
not mine to keep...

~*ap*~

may this be love
under the moon let it be me
where only luck comes slow
and the lord can only predict
inside of me has fragments that indicate the shattered clouds
and rains that sting my cheeks
wither in knots tightened by dreams for good times
this old world continues to turn
and make-believe that your love was pure
if only you knew i wouldn't let go
my heart remains cold
until our sun folds back all our yesterdays
i have lost so far
now you leave me on a search for exactly you
in fairness, i will slowly disappear
but how am i supposed to pretend
that i never want to be with you again
as i feather my fingers over someone else's back
it will be your constellations
i can find underneath our lonely sky...

~*ap*~

you hold my heart like a grenade
and only you can nurse my wounds to aide
with a noose too loose to die but frayed
the bullets sprayed
and all casualties stayed
so we joined the endless parade
to meet me back where my hearts death, i myself made
questions and answers of why i strayed
from that love who i've always prayed
would come back and cascade
i wouldn't have to had conveyed
or delayed what feels right
and not ruin and evade
she was pure and homemade
and portrayed that no one could ever upgrade
that sweet taste of her lemonade
i'm sorry i disobeyed
this reckless man is overplayed
surveyed and overstayed
so i call out to the angels i trade
to stop killing this poet
with bullies and being afraid...

~ap~

it was...

it wasn't the drips teetering on the edges of gush
it wasn't the purview of goosebumps in all their hindrance
to not let it all go
it wasn't the fingertip dancing
where my hands learnt to waltz in a quiver of completely you
it was your smell
i couldn't live without...

~*ap*~

jerry cordeiro

stop!
just put away the laundry later
put on your sweatpants
tie your hair in a bun and come over
let's have a fire, drink some wine
dance in the kitchen to old songs
and then more kisses

~ap~

how many scars did i justify
because i loved the knight
holding the sword...

~ap~

jerry cordeiro

how can i find
what i already had
that was everything
i ever needed...

~ap~

i'm gonna stand
on top of a mountain
made from all the dead
versions of myself...

~*ap*~

i noticed those tiny things about you
that nobody would care to know
like how many freckles there are
between your shoulders to your kiss
the answer is thirteen

~ap~

i was terrified to love her
for the fear of her hurting me was too torturous
i wouldn't be able to stay alive
if i had let her completely in
then completely out...

~*ap*~

her.o.ine

i could not live without
as i idealized the illusion
that i fall deep in love
with the softness of shadows
the dark i am no longer scared of
so now when my eyes fasten
it's only you that visits me in my sleep
i could live inside your skin
and in the corners of your lips
and on the edges of your hips
is where i would build my palace
soft skin walls
eyes like windows
and your beating heart my radio
all songs are metaphors of forever inside of you
with ridges imbedded in my tongue
from the erosion of my words

april's promises

i have written your name a thousand times
if my thoughts spit out paper
a poet without a pen
is a mouth without water
i hide under wings from the birds of prey
fearful of the journey and afraid of the purpose of day
inside a cobweb i wait restless for the bite of the widow
whose death punctures like love of a forbidden bite
as the clock kills us all slowly
minute by minute
you can't change time by holding time
like an ache from a promised kiss
that was only to be mine
i wake up and feel better
and in that certainty and clearness of purity
i want you back inside my fucking veins

~ap~

we met through pictures
and i spent years picturing us together
now i have put away your photo
in the pocket of my ripped faded jeans
and i capture a vision when i fall to my knees and snap
i shoot everyone who dares to try and love me
and lose focus of the wish
that was granted to me that day we met
and all i can imagine is a frame on top of your mantle
in the middle of your living room
with me inside of it
holding you so tight that it shows a forever
that photograph was what we waited for
forever a click of a button...
us... artists carefree
living inside dreams and kisses...

~*ap*~

it was the edges
they all were sharp as a shark's stock
forever in years all i've done was tread shallow
where over pilled doors that were in constant lock
i can't explain how our hold felt but to only say
it was nothing i've ever felt and won't any other day
i fell on entry
and i couldn't escape from the corner of her mouth
i would dream with eyes closed
i believe i won't stop foraging with hands of a gypsy i'll clasp
because freedom must begin for it to have a chance to last
it was her edges
smooth as an unseen ocean
where no one sees the calmness of her dance
for only the squint in her eyes could bend light
i'm sailing again with a pirate's thirst
for treasure only a beggar would refuse...

~ap~

jerry cordeiro

before the wind
i was in love with breath
before her whisper
and all the meanings of death
and long ago
before i knew how to sense
we must have met in another life
on either side of the fence
i chased forever
not knowing it was you
and tried to capture love
like the butterflies do

~ap~

her...

is the only word i ever needed to scream...

~ap~

find and float

the hourglass held all sand in grinding minutes
and fucked all seconds that i seeped time
he takes water from my eyes like a scorched traveller
who constantly believes in a mirage
a withering flower is what his dry eyes beautify
he was bitten by addictions to sadness
and he never realized i was his antidote
now... i am only ink on paper and a lost note
i'll write to the lonely traveller
where i hope this message in a bottle
will find him and float...

~ap~

april's promises

if you were my butterfly
i'd take you home
i would ask you to define forever
while teaching me your secrets to soar

~ap~

jerry cordeiro

i left before his wings were ready
now i will forever wonder about his wander...

~*ap*~

do you love me?
yes, every day that ends in why

~ap~

if my eyes could speak
they would tell you everything
that reminds me of you
like the smell of my pillowcase
and the truth of my dreams

~ap~

i will try and learn to love the sound of my feet
walking away from things not meant for me
we could have been exactly what we wanted
forever among the clouds of our dreams
this road that you left me on is unfamiliar to me
but the sky is the same one i've been gazing at all my life
now, i must teach myself to dream for one...

~ap~

i know he's feral
what if i let him go wild
will his gallops slowly trot on my lonely field
where the grass at our feet
would only remember the pressure of fate
would he come back to everything different
but the same desire to breathe us again
will his instincts sink like rain
knowing its way through dirt and ground
where the roots will awake and celebrate the arrival of grip
i will never forget the possibilities of his gypsy wings
how from a distance they are tranquil
but close they are chipped and torn just like me
and just like me
i won't stop flying wild underneath big dippers
and the cluster of stars that reflect off your eyes
in between the flames of fire

~ap~

i found a flower inside a war
a friendly fire
spit bullets of words
i never meant to rifle
i crawled in trenches
to have one last attempt
a lost soldier who died each time
he tried killing the thought of you

~*ap*~

i've pulled slivers from your hand
and bandaged wounds left from words unsaid
my heart shrink wrapped for later devour
in reminiscing all those touches that ricochet inside
you're an eternal bloom where flowers die
and seed more temptations that i need
if only can you solve this knot
because it wasn't supposed to go like that
the unnecessary worry has eluded my filth
i think the gods left behind answers to your calling soul
was i the man you wished for
or could i've learned how
i haven't shown you all the sides of diamonds
but stones that have been left unturned remain
i get lost when imagination plays
and i drift between the perfume and your skin
wanting to explore those pieces
that were left from others failed attempts
you should have told me all your thoughts
left none of them to be over piled
because your heart tries to remind you
when my arms are around
but this world continues to spin in directions
that haven't gone as planned
i will continue to pursue
like a butterfly
i will land

~ap~

incarcerated into us

we met and incarnated into us
i couldn't keep my eyes shut no more
for all the insides needed was exactly her
i was inserted in my intuition of her perception
nobody told me that you could die from a heartbroken life
nobody taught me to allow love in and keep it
i learnt early on that i feared being left, left in one spot
looking through windows and speaking to trees
praying to the lord i wish i had someone just for me
i see glasses of water empty
and you were supposed to fill my bucket
but when you dilute true love you change its form
and the function of your future is altered forever
now i'm an outlier
detached from being attached
to the soul mate that the magic was trying to prove
your wine dipped lips
my tongue lashing inside rum
in attempts to inebriate all organs that make me miss you
i don't just miss you, it's deeper than that
parts of me died and in no way could those stones mend
i'm opposed to compose the demise of my rose
because now you're a garden of thorns
we met and i am incarcerated into us

~ap~

i never in my entire
have fallen so wreaked
my sail blemished with torn wings
your eyes and my rebellious heart
cause stars to shatter under the same sky
i smirk and you smile in contrary motion
i ask birds to send you messages as you are my wonder
i'll pretend to hold you in evenings
that are late for my fantasies
i will picture your hands around my face
and places where clothes hide private things
are you dead to love again
or are you hungry for the real feel
in all my tiny broken pieces
i can resist all temptations but you
freedom is all i have
so stay
don't go

~ap~

everyone in the world wants the same as me
we want wild eyes and all the words they hold
how strange is it that after i see you
butterflies find their way back
deep through layers slightly above wounds
my existence can touch you in places where miracles settle
i'll be waiting for you
when you're changing slowly to the person you truly are
i'll search far
i will land on your island
and rescue you from the tired years
and crashing waves
your eyes are inside others
for their day you give clarity
but by night your skin may crawl over to me
in sand my gears they grind to all the thoughts of me
 inside that lonely tear that i crave and all the salt it holds

~ap~

jerry cordeiro

don't wait too long to make things right
i'm not going to chase the sky forever
i'm not going to be left on this rock
without trying to swim
your cold feet and my warm heart
will make sure the tears disguise in the storms
stop searching for the perfect symphony
and find the beauty in my mistakes
my waters are rough
and they will forever crash against your shores
hoping that i'll find you somewhere ready to build in sand
ready to be deserted in only complete hunger
for my hands to touch back
don't wait too long because when you come undone
who will repair?
all those feeling you would leave
and let fall will grow into vines
the deeper i crawl
the less i look for diamonds

~ap~

if you were my butterfly, i would take you home
i would ask you to define forever
while telling me your secrets to soar
that's where i would start
i would begin there
but i might end up on my knees, looking up at you
there is no deception in my squirm
and you will know that by how much my body hurts so good
the pain will be from wanting it more, wanting it all
i'll shiver at any thought of that stopping
will i need to open windows
allowing you to see that my jar is full
full of your breath and safe from false shadows
if you fly out, be careful
be careful with our wings
they are fragile and in several pieces
all scattered, in random, precious, gusts of hope
i've been waiting so long for me to change
that by watching you, i learn to crawl
give me all the reasons i need
and i'll give you a reason to breathe
against the storms you become clear to me
when my sky befriends the dark
don't go, unless we together
forget to fly...

~ap~

on the curve of my neck
the stains of tears have all poured like a child
that scratches his nails in a lonely sandbox
deep in my image
a careless pirouette spins inside my marrow
until torrential pain floods
choking a proud arrogance that puts you apart
you became an invisible dream
you never dared to touch my innocence
inside my torn pocket
i remember the pressure you pressed
love forces us to change our plans
it echoes out messages to the air
that leaves voices among the tall grass
i'll wait until the lengthening wings break
like brittle bones in a battle of bullets and fear
beautiful things made new
from the surprise of agony's colours
give me back my wings only on the way down
so i know the comfort of falling
like the last tear that stained

~ap~

i would taste deep and hoard yesterdays into piles
it feels like i could hold you in countless hours
laying in your arms and seeing all seasons change
your skin my fantasy
your insides my destiny
i tried to run from love
but like love songs they remained humming
if you had another chance with reckless desire
would you play in my battlefields of butterflies
with glass wings so we can see below
everything that held us back
from tasting deeper

~ap~

jerry cordeiro

everybody wants happiness
with minimal struggle to gain
but you can't learn to smile
without a little rainy pain

~ap~

if you fall in love with a poet
each poem you read
you will always wonder
if you own his pen and paper

~ap~

i'm jealous the wind gets to push through your hair
and the trees are left with the smell of your subtle sway
i've fallen for you
the same way feathers glide
when broken from a bird's journey
perhaps i have a plan that's better far for you
where yesterday was something i never thought of keeping
and today will pretend to be gone as soon as i go
keep me in the pockets of your mind
pull me out when you need to breathe
and place me gentle when you must feel
between your heart and your scars i will rest forever...

~ap~

i hit a good vein to let the truth cum out
i pulled without effort in my fingers
her loose thread detached and winced in agonizing thresh
i yank a bit more as i inhale all secrets reveal themselves
my feet are wet again
from her disciplined rain that i so much require to imbibe
i pluck at her with gentle touches from years of yearn
as it begins to unravel i initiate her warmth
her skin is like petals from flowers unseen
i wait patiently until denial reassures she was only a dream
she didn't exist
she was only my mind's way of finding adoration
i closed my new eyes and darkness fucked me slowly
i enjoyed being beaten
to all rhythm of her denied love for me
i must find the real her...

~ap~

jerry cordeiro

last night i dreamt of you again
this time
we were forever
where we were supposed to be
caught in love
inside dreams

~*ap*~

all we need is the simplest form of fixing
eye gazing, slowly touching hands
and catching each hidden piece
of everything we are...

~ap~

if anything, to hold
the lord warned me
not to let you slip through my hands
i wish
i wish he would have screamed like thunder
and awakened me from the calmness...

~ap~

wake up
babe...
i just had the worst dream
i dreamt we drowned in the ocean
of other people's opinions
we forgot how to swim
and most importantly we forgot
that we were raised to be wild
that we can never die underneath
crashing waves, landslides
and fires deliberately ignited
to blow away our ashes
wake me up...

~ap~

minutes before

slow down young moon in childish shine
living different lives in separate dreams
both sides now mirror the perfect scape
truth was missing
paper-thin in scriptures repaired
with no comprehension
come down now, because i tried my best
in creeks that turned deep and edgy
a very long goodbye and longer my thoughts sit
my heavy heart glides over clouds
where ideas of you are bottled at sea
your perfume sits still in memories gust
why should it still hurt but it must
our love was lost above
where wings and wind encounter

the possibilities you let fall grow into vines
smothering the growth of others to flint
i walk thoughtless with eyes keen ripping the seam
a mended mind stitched together
with strings played from spiders anxious to spin
a phase i faulted
fed up and full
you gave the last chance to fate's façade
which keeps my hostage in hostilities' hinges
the old will soothing in innocence and urgency
i send you my smile again
if my wings should fail me
for one brief spell i'd cast
to see you one last time
in minutes before

~ap~

deep inside every thought of you is a window
a window to the sky
as i picture your hair blowing in whispers
or windows in my dreams
there are windows in her eyes
making me plan the rest of existence
all of these thin sheets of glass have another side
where an invisible door is unlocked
and just you...
only you...
can swing over every cloud
and find exactly why windows are so necessary to open
let's fall together
and shatter each pain

~*ap*~

boil the ocean and take out the salt
strain the storm's tears especially if not your fault
poison the mouths of the politician's greed
and feed then unwillingly
if they assume what i need
clean their ears
so eyes could feel what resistance shoves
and teach old dogs
how to howl
to the moon for love...

~ap~

if he loved you true
his reflection would appear on the shattered glass at my feet
he would place his hand on my shoulder
and whisper, i love you
let's hold each other until we fall asleep
because tomorrow
i'll love you an extra 24 hours of truth...

~ap~

tranquility was brutally slain
as fading out to you enchantingly she casts
leaving a place not here not ever in her eyes
i was a favourite mistake
where falling moons promised her wish back
as i seize into the heart
i could only sweep the little things away
as special as each different star assembles in the daytime
the little tiny stones wearing down the same
on the sharp edges of my sole
so now... shattered sleeps are transcending
with the end of a passionate try
so be gentle with my heart as you hold it
because beyond tomorrow i fell so deep
into your seep
my exhausted sleep

~ap~

jerry cordeiro

forever as the end wouldn't exist
our love story of wishes
and burning skin
will forever live in my pen

~ap~

it was you
that was her
it was me
that wishes had arrived
if the gods of love
weren't ready to give up so easy
they would tell us we must
get through fire
to earn the scars
as soon as we
accepted fate
our lives would be
exactly as it should
forever under
white sheets
curled like vines
inside laughter
and wine

~ap~

eagles fly alone
they soar higher than the storms
and avoid the drenched feeling of being afraid
afraid of the unknown possibilities
that happiness might be around that mountain
after the storm pushes you down i'll bring the calmness back
i won't ever let you sit alone in wonder
i won't ever be lost in tall grass but a home i will build
we will dance in front of a window
careless of the downpour of others
you owe yourself the love you've given to the birds
you watered, you fed, you held, you let go
we are fragile
yet strong enough to see through walls
in a delicate dream i call for you
you answer eventually but it comes in the shape of a sunrise
i close my eyes tight so i hold you in my mind
you have found the one who will watch every sunrise
and who will hold every sunset in his hands
place your fingers in between his and in the morning
you'll be okay...

~ap~

i'd be forever for him
if only he would let me
but the pain of being left behind
is stronger than the scratches that bleed
i may have wished for him
to turn this soul to pure
goodbyes are hard to accept
but excruciating to endure

~ap~

how i think you could
if you gave me a chance i would
i was something you never understood
but you never saw the good
and it was all you ever should
all your riddles make me write my rhymes
all your broken pieces and all of mine grind
all my pain i try to keep caged
all fall on the paper with pen fucking rage
by leaving me you sharpened my sword
i allowed you to build castles of love
with shining nights that your gluttony hoards
i wanted something beautiful to die for
so i could live getting used to broken things
i could have tasted honey without getting stung
and the swarms of discomfort that follow your bring
i fondle the four-letter word
and make it bleed a letter at a time

cause these eyes you once could read turn to a waiting page
but plagiarism isn't the crime
my trust laid on your soul just like a vow unrehearsed
a slow descending, unending cycle
and now we must dry up our thirst
i own a big sky behind my house where dreams seem to lap
and forever is slightly above my smile
it wasn't the sweetness of your sap
the pale blue of your eyes
and the way our metals weld
in our arms no other could be properly held

~ap~

there's no need to rebuild
the bridges that we burnt
those good times were only to derail
and be hijacked by fear of new travels
but then sadness will linger
between us getting older
and all those gentle touches i knew to give, will rust
he won't know how
he won't know how to thrust in anticipations anatomy
they won't know how to enjoy soaking your tears
that poetically drop to the creases of my prints
he won't enjoy the claw marks as much as my eagle mind
the dew you let out will dry
and i won't ever get close enough to wet my palate
this time it feels different from the rest
the emptiness is settling with words i let out paper-thin
your skin doesn't burn because my fire is out
i will miss you in eternity's torment
all i have is a window i could see through
and a door i can close
the fail of facing our fears is what our relationship chose
and every shooting star will just make me close my eyes
because as much as i try to replace
it will be you that lives in all my skies

~ap~

please don't wait too long
because you will lose nothing less than everything

~ap~

jerry cordeiro

you're so vain
you probably
think these poems
are about you
don't ya?

~*ap*~

we were gazing madly
to find a sign
that would remind us
that we once carried
magic potions in our kiss
a shooting star spoke
of our twin flame
and inside my lifeless body
i was puzzled into your scattered pieces
perfectly placed
in the constellations
of a midnight sky

~*ap*~

the immortality of these pages
will sail on like a ship
carelessly lost in timeless oceans
where you can lose yourself
in others' symptoms of sorrow
books are the reason we believe in god
all the voices from everything dead
have now seen heaven
and they all just wrote about it
likewise, this lonely poet
with eyes shut and tilted to the sun
dreams about indescribable adventures
that my words and thoughts
could fall in love forever
all over again and again and again

~ap~

jerrycordeiro.com

To order more copies of this book, find books by other
Canadian authors, or make inquiries about publishing
your own book, contact PageMaster at:

PageMaster Publication Services Inc.
11340-120 Street, Edmonton, AB T5G 0W5
books@pagemaster.ca
780-425-9303

catalogue and e-commerce store
PageMasterPublishing.ca/Shop

jerry cordeiro

with a laundry basket filled with jagged pieces
of paper, scrunched up napkins and ripped
out pages of other books, jerry cordeiro began
writing years ago for a way of releasing the
burden of holding feelings in. poetry has been
a way to balance the dexterity of his thoughts.
this first book is only just love letters, the first
of many stained pages to come. if a poet has
written poetry on the edges of his fingertips
and the ridges of her skin, then his words will
fall in eternity's love affair with death.

april's promises volume one.
instagram @aprils_promises
jerrycordeiro.com